WHITE MOCS ON THE RED ROAD
WALKING SPIRIT IN
A NATIVE WAY

WHITE MOCS ON THE RED ROAD

WALKING SPIRIT IN
A NATIVE WAY

By

James B. Beard

Edited by
Noreen Powers

DEDICATION

This book is dedicated to my teacher, Nagaan we widong, [na-gaan-way-wi-dong / First to Speak, First Thunder, Lawrence Joe Matrious, A man who dedicated his life to the people. An Elder of the Ojibwe Nation of People that live around the great lakes in North America. His teachings, patience and example changed my life and that of many others who knew him. He was one of the last of the Old Ones of Lake Lena Reservation in Hinckley, Minnesota. I say here that he was one of the last, though in truth he is one of the old ones. Though he passed on August 9th, 2009, he is still with us in spirit and continues to affect my life on a daily basis.

ACKNOWLEDGEMENT

Larry Matrious – Mishomis, my teacher, brother, guide to all that has become in my life. To thank you would be too shallow. To carry your message to others is the call that I hear. It is a way to honor you and all that you are. Miigwich!

Brian Matrious – All of the art in this book is your work. Your art expresses the true meaning given by Spirit. My brother, medicine man, helper. Everything in this book honors you for being who you are. Without the time that we have traveled, I would never have understood what I know to be true of Spirit and man. Miigwich!

Medewiwin Lodge – My life is dedicated to you! All that I do is to support the teachings of spirit that flow through you. In gratitude to you I offer all that I am to help others to know and understand the work of the lodge. Miigwich!

Peter Schuler – My brother, sponsor and guide. You, who taught me the importance of tobacco and have stood by me when I thought even fools would be wise enough to walk away. Your wisdom knows no bounds and what is offered here could not have been said without your help and support. Miigwich!

Austin Miximong – My brother by adoption, clan and all that connects us to all things. I walked for a time on this path, not knowing who I was. At one fire in one moment you changed my life. Miigwich!

Eddy Miximong - My brother by adoption, clan and all that connects us to all things. Your smile invited me to the fire. You showed me how to laugh and brought me back to the child within me. My life would not be my life without what you have given. Miigwich!

Maize – Are you man or spirit? In my heart I know! Migwich my Haudenosaunee Elder. As you approached I was groping for direction. As you walked on I understood the path that is my life. I will look forward to when I see you again.

Monica Beard – My wife and fellow spirit visitor. Yes! I know who you are! Thank you for all that you gifted me in the years we traveled together. Thank you also, for setting me free. I will always love you and will come if you are in need.

Carol Beard – My wife, my friend. All the time that we have had was growth to become who we are today. Watching you live your life over these years since we parted has been a joy. I have you to thank for much of what I have come to know.

Charles-Nicholas Beard – My son and, I am thankful to say, my friend. I have given to you and you have given to me much over your life. You are the energy that has kept me balanced to stay in a place long enough to know it and I am grateful.

Stephanie Beard – I have learned so much from you. You are my youngest and most daring of my children. Your zest for life is an example of living life to the fullest. As I witness your love of life and all that surrounds you I find gratitude that you inspire for all that is. You are the Hawk in heart that surrounds you.

Meagan Beard - Spirit walks close to you and I have witnessed that in you since long before I understood what I have come to believe in this time. Even as a child things would happen to you and it would seem as if some strange protector surrounded you. In this time you have learned to accept that protector and know that you are safe. You are an inspiration.

Kathryn Lyn Skulley – Your energy. Your joy of life. Your ability to overcome all obstacles with complete determination. Your walk of beauty in this life is such a blessing to see. The gift of the book "Wounded Knee" that impacted me so greatly. All of these things and more make the blessing of you a treasure in my life.

The Elders – My teachers, grandfathers, grandmothers and guides. There are so many of you now. At first I thought there could only be one and then later, just a few. You are teaching me daily of a life of beauty and respect. You show me in so many ways how to be the man that I am. I can only honor you in one way. I will do the work! Miigwich!

CONTENTS

PREFACE

Some things in life happen that one could never foresee. The story you are about to read is about one of those things. Like most people, my life was pretty well laid out for me. Growing up in a small town in western New York, going to school, serving in the military, getting a job, getting married and raising a family. The typical American dream.

The walk that follows was so far from my path that I doubt anyone even twenty years ago would have guessed that it would be how I would spend the rest of my life. My past wives and family knew me, as did my peers, as a business man and one who was vested in my community in Southern New Hampshire. Serving on boards of non profits, going to Rotary, doing Chamber of Commerce functions and running an insurance agency were a part of what I saw as my whole life. I was a three piece suit.

What would come to be was never intended in my mind. In a time of transition, I began to look for answers about living that seemed to be missing in my life. It seemed as if the fulfillment of the promise of the American dream was somehow incomplete. I began to look for something to fill in the missing pieces. As I searched for that missing part I almost literally stumbled on the first people of this land. As I began to learn of their continued existence, they led me on an extraordinary path of understanding. These people who I did not even know still existed, continue to have the gifts of a beautiful culture that respects all things. The goal for me then became to find those gifts.

With the history between the original people of this land and the people who have more recently come here, it can be difficult to gain an understanding of the depth of the teachings within the culture of the Native American Indian. The trust level is understandably not there. The oral teachings carried by the Elders are not openly shared with just anyone who would ask.

The original intent of my quest was to gain new insight and add it to my existing life. It was not to change my lifestyle or relationships. What came about began to take me from the life I had known and to begin an adventure into a different world. I found myself in transition to a person that I did not know existed within myself. My white heritage would be enhanced by the ancient teachings that we all once had. I would learn to wear white moccasins to walk a red road in order to better understand the original teachings of my own people. The path that I would follow would give me a new family, a new community to be a part of and a new identity beyond anything I could have imagined. The life style, values and dedication of my life would now change for the rest of my time. To all of this I can only say, miigwich! thank you!

INTRODUCTION

At the time of this writing many years have passed doing the work of the people. The life that I live has transcended from the daily hobble down city streets seeking to make a living to a life dedicated to helping others. In the work that I now do I am a helper to others and in following each day I make the effort to address what is there in the moment.

My first teacher, Larry Matrious a.k.a. Nagan We Widung a.k.a. First to Speak a.k.a. First Thunder, is an Ojibwe Indian of the Potowatomy Tribe. He lives in Minnesota along the St. Croix River and visits periodically in the Northeastern United States. Larry, who I address as Misho, has been my teacher for many years. He lives far away and we would only visit periodically in the early years of my learning from this man.

Often in recent years Larry and I would meet and discuss the things I was learning and how they were applicable in my life. The dialogue of this story is true as best I remember. Since we were not in touch on a daily basis, there were many parts of my growth that needed telling so that he could respond to my questions and understanding.

Most of the time he was very compassionate with me but there were also times when he would become totally frustrated with my lapses in understanding.

Larry has lived in two ways through his life. He was raised on a reservation in the old way in his early years. He went into the service when he was young and served during the Korean conflict and was a champion light weight boxer. He followed the Christian faith for many years while living in St. Paul, Minnesota and was a musician. In his life he eventually returned to the reservation and began to live the traditional ways of his people.

His wisdom and insight is humble and unassuming but when he enters a room everyone will feel his presence. This is a man dedicated to helping Spirit and all people and looking with love on the people of his nation. As Larry will tell you, he is an Indian.

All that is the culture of the Native American Indian is not open to just anyone who comes searching. People ask questions and want to assume so much, so fast, that the depth of teachings of the Indian is often missed entirely. One does not just decide to follow native teachings and pick up a pipe, a feather, run a sweat lodge, do a ceremony, be a medicine man or become a chief. These and many other parts of the culture and teachings of the Native American Indian take a lifetime of learning and dedication to Spirit and the people in order to do, or to understand. It is a heritage that only an Indian can truly share and no one but another Indian would ever totally relate to.

The beauty is that what they can share is beneficial to all. After all, we are all related. All of our ancestors once had the same teachings. Lest we forgot.

I am new to this way and know nothing of my own. I have been gifted with the guidance of many teachers over the years. To receive this gifting required total dedication to helping and serving the people. Watching, listening and doing the work are the ingredients to learn the ways of Spirit and the people. In time, one day, sometimes after years of coming around, an Elder will look at you and say, "build me a fire." Now you have begun to learn.

CHAPTER ONE

While We Were Dancing

~ *Debwe win* ~ **[truth] Understand** all that is of those things that you use. Truth is the completeness of understanding of what is. Be true to yourself and true to your fellow man. Always speak the truth.

"What do you want me to do?" Noodin asked.

Misho was slow to answer as they sat in the car in the rain. The wind was blowing hard and they could feel the car rock with each gust of the air. It was a good time to talk. It was not a good time to get out of the vehicle.

"Keep doing what you are doing now. Remember I will always speak to you honoring the seven gifts. I expect the same from you," Misho answered.

"I honor that. I have since I first came to know you."

"What do you know about Ju-di-ism from Ireland?" Misho asked.

"Ju-di-ism? Nothing! I don't know what that is. Do you mean Druidism[1]?"

"No. I think it is Ju-di-ism and it is also in Egypt and Europe and England," Misho replied.

Noodin answered, "I think you mean Druidism and it doesn't seem to me that there is much to know. Most of the teachings are lost. Bits and pieces of information were passed down through some families in Europe but even those teachings have been melded into myth over the years. What is written was recorded by Christian monks from 800AD to 1100 AD. The Christian monks regarded the Druids as heathens and an enemy to the people, so nothing that they wrote about them was particularly flattering. What I have read tells mostly war stories about a brutal and uncivilized people. The Druids were the priests of the Celtic and/or Gaul people. Is that who you are speaking about?"

"Yeah! I guess so", said Misho.

"It is not so important that I am Ojibwe. That is just my tribe. I am an Indian. That is what is important, that I am an Indian. That is who I am!"

Misho is short for Mishomis, the Ojibwe word that translates as Grandfather. Noodin addresses him as Misho. Noodin's teacher is Nagaan way Wedung [Na-gaan-way-we-dong] in Ojibwe. He is a slight man with dark amber colored skin that is well weathered. His name means 'first thunder' or 'he who speaks first' in the language of the Ojibwe[2]. He is only about five foot five inches tall now but was probably taller in his younger years. He kind of looked Indian but not like the Indians Noodin had envisioned as a boy. He was born in the bush along the St Croix River in Minnesota and he is between seventy and eighty years old at this time. There is no record of his birth and his family hid him from the authorities when he was young so that he would not be taken to the Indian schools and removed from them.

Nish Nung, Misho's son, has taken Noodin to the place where Misho was born. It is a beautiful piece of land down by the river where a gentle bend curves the river into a long slow flow at a shallow place. There are two great tamarack pine trees that stand about twenty five feet

---

[1] Druidism - an ancient Celtic religion in which the forces of nature were worshiped, and the priests were also prophets and poets, or the modern religion said to derive from it.

[2] Ojibwe - a Native North American people who originally lived in the northeastern part of North America. The Ojibwe migrated from the eastern Algonquin language speaking tribes of the northeastern coastline over a thousand years ago.

apart where Misho was born in a small lodge built between them at a place close to the river. It is a place called the crossing and was a place in the river where the water is slowed and shallow making it easy to afford a crossing to the other side. It is where the people of the Cross Roads Band [Azhaamook] of Ojibwe, had lived for hundreds of years.

"I understand Misho."

There was a pause.

Then Misho asked slowly and deliberately; "Who are you?"

Always direct questions from this man, Noodin's teacher.

The rain started coming down even harder as if it were making some sort of statement to emphasize the importance of the question.

"I am just a man." Noodin felt as if he had yelled it out to be heard over the rain. He knew that was not what Misho wanted to hear. Misho was making a point and Noodin avoided it.

"I hate when he confronts me with a direct question," Noodin thought. "I never feel that I will give an answer that will be right even when there are really no wrong answers."

Misho looked down at the floorboard of the car with some dismay. The wrinkles on his face went deep with concern about how to say the next thing he would share. It was a full minute before he said anything.

The rain fell back to a light patter and Misho spoke softly.

"You need to search for your own bundle, Noodin. We share these things to help you find that direction. Here is an article about a man who is a Druid."

He took a piece of paper from his pocket and handed it to Noodin.

"You should call him." Misho continued. The man says in this article that he is a third degree Druid and that there is a whole group of these people honoring their original teachings."

Noodin looked at the article briefly and put it in his pocket. "I will read it and check it out Misho," He answered.

The rain suddenly stopped. It was as if someone had turned a handle and shut it off.

Misho got out of the car and went into the house. He would be leaving New Hampshire in the morning to return to his home in Minnesota.

What was he trying to tell me? Noodin wondered to himself.

Everything that Noodin had learned from Misho had been gathered and given with the intent of helping him find out about himself. He felt he should have answered Misho more honestly. He should have told him who he is, who he has become, and the truth of what he has found out about himself from the teachings of this man, Misho.

Noodin has hung on every word given by this man. He has found that the basic wisdom shared with him offered balance and centering beyond anything that he could have ever imagined. This new way of life surpassed all of his greatest expectations.

Any man could answer 'I am just a man'. What a foolish answer and yet still a basic truth. The question of who you are seems so simple when put in terms the way Misho put it. The answer is also very complex in that it takes in the "all" of who one really is.

On the surface it seems to be a trivial question for one to ask another when you already know them, and Misho knows Noodin pretty well. It has been years learning from Misho to be at the place where Noodin has come to be.

Yes! Noodin thought. I know who I am!

Misho seemed to want him to say he is a white man from Europe or a Celt or a Druid. To Noodin all of these things are true but they alone do not describe Noodin. The transcendence that Noodin had undergone over the last years learning from Misho and others had indeed made a change. The question of "who is Noodin?" is not so simple as, "I am a white man".

Misho is an Indian! That is who he is. At least 95% because Noodin knew that many generations ago Misho had an ancestor that was a French Portage. Misho mentioned that one time in a gathering talking circle.

Who is Noodin? He is a white man who has transcended to a different cultural teaching. He is a man first named Jim. He is a man of ancient Celtic descent. Noodin is Noodin.

Noodin had learned an important fact from Misho over time. Everyone has a bundle, a collection of all that is who they are and all that they come to understand.

"Why couldn't I answer my teacher," Noodin wondered? Misho's first teaching was that you must always tell a person who you are when you meet them so that they know who they face.

Noodin indizhinikaz, maang indodiem, anishinabe bamaagaana, ogichidaa indow, Celtic indow! [Wind is how I am known, Loon is my clan, Indian it is that I am by adoption, it is that I am a veteran, I am Celt]

In past years Misho spent a lot of time in New England. His visits here have been fewer over the last couple of years. He remarried and his new bride, Noreena, didn't like to travel away from the rez except to go to powwows.

When he would come in the past he would stay for months at a time in New Hampshire. Every week he would conduct teaching circles to help anyone that would come. His circle was large. Many people would come to learn from this elder of the Ojibwe. Some were Native American and others were people that feel connected in spirit and wished to learn.

This was a time before Noodin knew Misho. When Noodin came to the circle, the gathering was only a remnant of the circle that had been. When Misho stopped coming to New England the circle began to shrink and separate into splinter groups. Misho had asked his adopted son, Oshki, to keep the circle alive but it was difficult to do this and still work in the dominant world we live in today. Oshki did what he could but found it overwhelming to maintain a circle following and to meet the other demands that were called for in his life.

A few months after the visit where Noodin was asked who he is, Misho came back to New England with his son, Nish Nung. Nish Nung was looking to develop some work for Misho and himself teaching about native traditional life to Indians here in the east. Misho is a well known elder of the Ojibwe people and could be of benefit to native people in New England that seek to understand their traditional culture and teachings. Much of what was the culture of the northeastern American Indian has been lost in the meld of the indigenous peoples with the new dominant society of the white man over the past five hundred years. The Ojibwe people still carry much of the original teachings that were known prior to their migration from the northeast over eight hundred years ago. Nish Nung also carries those teachings and is knowledgeable about medicines as well.

Noodin would join Misho and Nish Nung in Connecticut as guests of the Mashantucket Pequot Tribal Council[3]. Nish Nung was working on a plan to introduce traditional teachings to the youth group of the tribe. He had arranged meetings with the Pequot Tribal Council and they would leave New Hampshire to visit the Pequot Tribe in

---

[3] Mashantucket Pequot - a member of a Native North American people of eastern Connecticut. The tribe is active in reclaiming cultural teachings that are common to their ancestry.

Mashantucket, Connecticut in the morning. They would be in Mashantucket for four days and their lodging had been reserved for them by the council.

There is never much notice when Nish Nung and Misho are coming. A phone call in the middle of the night and news that they will arrive in a day or two is the norm.

Nish Nung asked Noodin to join them to be a helper, skabewis, during the meetings and ceremonies that would occur. They would stay at the Pine Tree Inn at Foxwoods Casino. Misho and Nish Nung would stay in one room and Oshki, Misho's adopted son, would share a room with Noodin.

Oshki and Noodin are skabewisug [ska-bay-wis ug / helpers] to Misho and Nish Nung in the native tradition. When Misho and Nish Nung travel east they look to Oshki and Noodin to make arrangements and to assist in ceremonies and meetings. As helpers, they make sure that the preparations are made and drop everything that they can of what they are doing to accommodate Misho and Nish Nung.

The one thing on Noodin's schedule that could not be put aside was a commitment to do a workshop in Rochester, New Hampshire on a Tuesday night of that week. In order to go to Connecticut Noodin would have to travel there and then leave from Connecticut to go to Rochester to do the workshop and then return to Connecticut.

A martial arts program in Rochester had asked Noodin to do a workshop on the medicine wheel. This was to be the third presentation in a series. There is no charge for the workshop but donations would at least cover the gas for the trip. The program would consist of teachings as they have been given to Noodin by Misho. In this time, this is Noodin's life work and it is given out as it was given to Noodin, in a sharing manner.

On the first day in Mashantucket, Nish Nung did an opening ceremony at an aboriginal language conference.

The gathering the four of them were attending was scheduled at the Mashantucket/Pequot Museum to address the preservation of the Algonquin Language and the development of a dictionary of the language. Many aboriginal people and scholars were gathered to discuss the manner that was used to develop a written dictionary of the language of the Ojibwe. Ironically, no Ojibwe people were invited to participate in the gathering. The presenters were anthropologists and professors that had conducted research. Some of the research had coincidentally been obtained from Misho but the people there did not know that. It was simply a matter of timing that we happened to be there at the time of this program.

The ceremony Nish Nung would do was to ask for Spirit guidance for this gathering and he would do this with a pipe ceremony to offer prayers for the event. Noodin's work was to assist Nish Nung in this ceremony. Nish Nung had been invited to do the ceremony by the Mashantucket/Pequot Council as a last minute thought to honor the program being given.

Nish Nung then would have meetings with the Pequot Indian Council all day.

After the ceremony Misho and Noodin spent the day looking around the museum at Foxwoods.

The museum is an amazing collection of artifacts with a brief history of the people. Most of the history has to do with the ways the people have lived and developed over the last several hundred years. There is a replica of the villages that were lived in by the people and a lot of information on the history of conflict between the colonists and King Philip, a chief of the Pequot people.

An interesting presentation about the holding of the land by a few native Pequot people describes how some families stayed on the land to maintain possession. When recognition was gained from the United States government it was critical to have this land occupied by the original inhabitants. The efforts of the few who remained made it possible for the claim to tribal rights of land, and provided a place for the people of the Pequot line to return to when they were called back to establish their tribal rights.

The only thing lacking is any description of their traditions, ceremony and clans. Most of that has been lost in their history.

When they left the museum Noodin and Misho returned to their rooms to rest.

As mid-afternoon approached Noodin went to Misho's room to let him know he was leaving for Rochester. A snow storm was expected and Noodin would need to leave right away. Nish Nung had returned from his meetings and was sitting in the room when Noodin entered.

"I have to get going," Noodin announced; "It will take three hours to get to Rochester from here and maybe longer with the storm and all."

"Ok!" Nish Nung said. "Hey! Why doesn't my Dad go with you? It will give you two a chance to visit."

Noodin was hoping Nish Nung wouldn't suggest that. Misho had never seen him do a presentation and Noodin didn't want the criticism that he was sure would follow. Misho has taught Noodin most of what Noodin knows and he could not help but feel a little intimidated when in Misho's presence. The thought of presenting with Misho in the room made Noodin feel nervous. Noodin guessed that he lacked confidence about the knowledge he had received from Misho, but he really did not want to face that. Noodin always felt that Misho was skeptical of his dedication to native teachings. In the years that Misho had been Noodin's teacher the two of them never really got to be close. Noodin came to the circle for teachings after Misho had gone to live back in Michigan. Misho never knew Noodin as well as the others in the band of people here in New England.

"It is a long trip and there won't be much for Misho to do," Noodin protested.

Nish Nung persisted; "He will have a chance to see how you present your work and the two of you will have time to visit. I am going out with Aaron tonight anyway so this way my Dad will have company."

Aaron Looking Bear, an Apache, was a liaison with the Mashantucket Pequot Museum and assigned to host Misho and Nish Nung while at Mashantucket.

"I don't mind going along for the ride," Misho interjected. "There isn't anything for me to do here. Let's get going! Umbe aye!"

CHAPTER TWO

The Real Question

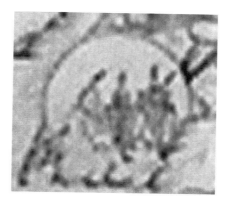

~**Miishiikenh**~ [turtle] Turtle carries the land we live on and the truth of all knowledge.

Misho and Noodin got into Noodin's car and began the drive to Rochester, New Hampshire from Mashantucket, Connecticut. Rochester is where Noodin would do the workshop. Of the three part series, tonight was to be on the Seven Gifts and Prophesy.

"Mino giizhi gut, [mi-no-gee-zhi-gut / it is a good day], it is a good day!" Misho said, to make conversation.

"Yes, I just hope the weather is okay all the way up to Rochester," Noodin answered.

"It will be Okay. We'll make it." Misho said.

There was a pause and then Misho said; "What made you follow these ways Noodin?"

Noodin began to tell his story.

"Wow! I guess it began twenty four years ago when I bottomed out on alcohol and went into AA. I was raised in the Episcopal Church and was active in the church up to that time as a Lay Reader and Sunday School Teacher. I was even training to become a deacon of the church. It was good for my insurance business and I basically believed that there was something to the religious part of it. I never questioned what I believed very much. You know?"

Misho; "so you are a Christian by belief right?"

"Well, I was at that time in some ways. It was my bringing up," Noodin answered.

Noodin continued; "When I went to AA and started to work the recovery program, the people attending meetings told me I needed to do a moral inventory of my life and then share it with another human being and God, as I understood him. I went to meetings every day and worked hard to understand my life. I realized that my understanding of a power greater than myself was really pretty shallow.

After being in the program for a while, I decided that I needed to get more in touch with my religion and faith in this higher power I was beginning to know. I began to attend church in Lakewood, Colorado. The same place I attended church before I started recovery in AA. I knew people there and felt that it would be a good place for me to be. When I began attending again, the church was the same but I was different than before, for some reason. I didn't feel like I was part of that family anymore and kind of felt out of place there. The people were kind enough and glad to see me back but I didn't feel comfortable. I couldn't put my finger on it but something had changed. I was finding out things about myself in sobriety and beginning to question information that I had basically taken for granted in the past. You know, to do with my spiritual beliefs.

This feeling of not being a part of this church was puzzling to me. I was very strongly indoctrinated to the Episcopal Church. My family went to church every Sunday when I was growing up. I attended a private Episcopal School, Shattuck in Faribault, Minnesota as a teenager. As a young man I had become a lay reader and Sunday school teacher in the church. Not to feel comfortable in this place I had grown up as a part of didn't seem to make sense. Something in coming to sobriety and looking at my life had engendered a change in the way I saw things.

Some things I questioned had to do with childhood memories of silly incidents that occurred when I was learning about the Christian religion I was raised in. Like one time in Sunday school when I was about seven or eight. The teacher was talking about how Jesus walked on the water. I asked her how Jesus did that. How did he walk on water? I felt that I was asking a valid question but the teacher thought

I was being some kind of smart ass. She retorted, "it is what happened and you just accept that as fact. Now you go stand outside of the room for the rest of the class". I didn't ask a whole lot of questions after that, but I always wondered how I was supposed to accept things I don't understand.

Other questions I had in coming back to the church were a little more important to me. I was beginning to question the basic intent and history of this religion I had been raised to accept. What do the other religions say? Is there some basic truth that lies at the basis of all spiritual understanding? Do all religions have a history of missionary work to push their beliefs? Are they all filled with a history of bloodshed and persecution of those who are so called non-believers and those that are martyrs of their belief? Isn't there more to spirituality than man as the master under God and the world as a place for us to dwell? I wasn't feeling real comfortable with the things I was being told I must believe to be a part of this religious group, the Episcopal Church. At this point the Christian faith in general became doubtful in my mind.

I thought about what I basically believe and determined I believe that we are all connected somehow. That nature, the universe and life on this planet all are integrally intertwined with each other. That there must be a higher power who has a part in all of this mystery of life. That all religious belief has a basic common denominator and that the denominator has nothing to do with I am right and you are wrong. Other than that I basically could not really say much about what I believe. I only knew I was uncomfortable in the church I had always called home and that something did not feel right to me.

There are so many books about faith, spirituality and religion. Everyone has something to say. I began to read about Spiritualism[4], Gnosticism[5], Judaism[6], Buddhism[7], Zen Teachings[8], Muslim[9] and

---

[4] Spiritualism - the philosophical doctrine that all reality is spiritual, not material.

[5] Gnosticism - a pre-Christian and early Christian religious movement teaching that salvation comes by learning esoteric spiritual truths that free humanity from the material world, believed in this movement to be evil

[6] Judaism - the religion of the Jews, which has its basis in the Bible and the Talmud. In Judaism, God is the creator of everything and the source of all goodness.

[7] Buddhism - a world religion or philosophy based on the teaching of the Buddha and holding that a state of enlightenment can be attained by suppressing worldly desires.

[8] Zen Teachings - a major school of Buddhism originating in 12th-century China that emphasizes enlightenment through meditation and insight.

[9] Muslim - relating to the followers of Islam or to areas, cultures, or activities in which followers of Islam are especially numerous.

many other beliefs. Anything I could find. The more I read the more I realized that they all fundamentally pointed to the basis of love as a fundamental teaching centered within all of them. The closest thing to anything I felt comfortable with, at least for the time being, was spiritualism and it seemed like that concept still had a lot of absolutes people have expressed as a condition of understanding. Why do people always have to say it can only be valid if it is their way?

So I would be a spiritualist and walk around this world knowing I believe in a spiritual acceptance of my creator and the relationship of that to do with all things. Great! Probably there are millions of spiritualists out there. We all walk around, comfortable that we have an understanding of our belief. We pass each other on the street; do business with one another, watch each other sitting in restaurants, alone, and we find comfort in the fact that there are many of us who believe this way.

The problem is who are all these people? How can we get together and learn from one another so we can grow in our understanding? Well, sometimes in a conversation we kind of get in touch with one another. I believe this. Says I. Oh? So do I really, but I am a Methodist. He or she says. Then we go on with our important little lives and forget about it.

On Sundays I might go to one church or another, maybe a mosque or a synagogue just to pray with some other people, or maybe just to be around other people. I don't know. Perhaps it was just my curiosity to see how these places worked.

As years went on I divorced and remarried. I tried to find a church that the new wonderful light in my life and I could enjoy together. We both had been raised Episcopal so of course we were married and our two children, Charles-Nicholas and Stephanie were baptized in that church. My bride was spiritual, more like me, than religious and no church ever seemed to be just right for either of us. The problem with this spiritualism thing is that you never really know if you and the other person understand the same thing. It is nice not to have any rules to follow though. As our marriage bloomed and flowered it eventually came to a time when it began to shrivel. My wonderful light wanted to leave and divorce was the new issue.

I reached out more to my spiritual understanding for strength. Kind of, Oh God, help me now, kind of thing. I started to go back to church at the Episcopal Church in New Hampshire where we now lived. "If you want to be happy and live with me, we need to live in

New Hampshire". I'll never forget when she said that, years before. She says she never said it but that is what I heard in my heart. She is probably the only person in the world who could have persuaded me to move away from Colorado.

It wasn't unusual for me to go to church and be a spiritualist. Most of my fellow spiritualists are there, though they may not admit they are spiritualist. Have to follow the flock, you know. I would go and say the prayers in the prayer book and sing the songs in the hymnal and listen to the readings and the sermon. Say hello to everyone and smile at them while I made my weekly pilgrimage to acknowledge God. Sunday is a good day for God, lots of admirers.

Then there was the Sunday I went to church and sat in the pew toward the back. A place I usually occupied to be inconspicuous, sitting by myself. My shriveling family was not into this church thing. The processional hymn began and the priest and choir and the entire processional came down the aisle dressed in their robes. I looked around at all of the beauty that is the history of this church where I had been raised and wondered at the splendor of the service. The mahogany pews and arched ceilings with ornate chandelier lamps hanging from the high ceilings make it a special place of solemn respect to the Lord.

The priest said the introductory prayer and then called for the parish to recite the Nicene Creed[10]. I began with the rest. "I believe in the Father, the Son and the Holy Ghost...", then, I suddenly stopped. I stood there as the people continued and I thought. That is all I really believe of this creed.

I remembered that a part of my recovery from alcohol depends on being thoroughly honest with myself, all people and my God as I understand him, her or it, whatever. Here I am standing reciting that I believe something that I do not believe to be true in my heart. How can I say "one holy Catholic and apostolic church" when I do not believe that and still be thoroughly honest with myself and the Creator?

I put the prayer book back in its shelf and walked out of the church. I never went back. I needed to be more diligent in seeking the truth as I understand it and to be honest with myself about what I believe when it comes to my relationship with creator.

---

[10] Nicene Creed - a formal statement of Christian beliefs formulated at a council held in Nicaea in ad 325, subsequently altered and expanded, and still in use in most Christian churches.

It was Christmas in that year that I received a gift from my oldest daughter, Kathy, in Colorado. She gave me a book called "Bury My Heart at Wounded Knee" by Dee Brown. It is an American history of the Native American. I thought it was nice and put it aside to read later. It sat for several months on the table in the living room before I finally picked it up and began to read a little from it. As I began to read, I found it to be compelling and I could not seem to put it down. I would often be brought to tears to read of the outlandish things that happened and the atrocities that occurred on both sides of this sad event that was unfolding. This history of how our ancestors, native and non-native inter-related to develop this country and this continent.

I would think as I read some of the histories, these things sound right, but they aren't the way I remember being told of them when I went to school. I remembered how the settlers had to forcefully take the land or be wiped out by the Indians. Kind of the John Wayne, good guy, Indians, bad guy attitude that was more prevalent when I was growing up in the fifties.

After reading the book I was puzzled enough about the difference to go and check some more recently published history books that were in the library. "My God!" I thought to myself; "They rewrote the whole thing since I was a kid." The modern books related a similar story to "Bury My Heart at Wounded Knee".

There is something else I noticed as I read "Bury My Heart at Wounded Knee". There seemed to be something that gave the Indian an ability to survive and even conquer against enormous odds. Something more than just defending their land and families. We all thought we were doing that. They would go into battle and it would cost five to ten American soldiers lives to take one Indian life. They had something. A belief it seemed. They had a belief that was so strong and continual in their manner of living that they could survive against unbelievable odds. They seemed to know something in their belief system that gave them strength. I thought of what my Dad used to say was his motto from Sir Galahad, "My strength is of the strength of ten because my heart is pure". They had that!

I had never considered the Indian as spiritual or necessarily good hearted. How could I have missed that? Everything that I knew was based on the idea that their beliefs weren't much more than good stories to tell to kids. Indians were colorful, resourceful, nature minded, brutally warrior like and of course, defeated. They were a defeated people who had lost their pride and will to a dominating society. They sat on reservations and waited for "we the tax payers" to send them money and supplies while they complain that we don't live up to the treaties that we agreed to. It was that "I'm right, you're wrong" thing creating a barrier between the cultures so that no one would really want to know much about each other. Now I was seeing a whole new people in the Indian. A people I never knew existed."

"So the book was the door that started you in this direction?" Misho interjected.

"No! I wouldn't say that." Said Noodin. "It gave me an awareness that prepared me to accept this direction but I wouldn't say that I was at the door yet. You might say I was standing on the porch.

I had a dream around that time. Going through my shrinking marriage I found I was having several dreams that were not so happy. This one was different though. Most of my dreams are not unique and I usually don't remember enough about them to make any big deal over them. For whatever reason, I had a Technicolor dream.

In the dream I saw a man standing in the middle of a long straight road. He was wearing a bright red vest and a top hat that was also bright red and made of straw. I looked around. I was standing in front of an old dilapidated log cabin with a porch and a wood plank walk that went up to the road where the man was standing. On the porch there were several dogs, a goat and cats.

I asked the man what he was doing and he answered; "I am going to take this house." I responded; "You can't take the house." He replied; "Why not?" I said; "You can't take the house because no one is home and I won't let you."

The next thing I know, I am lying on top of a stack of firewood on that porch and the dogs and cats are lying around and on top of me. I heard something around the back of the house. I got up and looked in the back. There was a fenced field and in it there was a buffalo and a goat. Both were wrapped from head to toe with thick rope and all I could see was the shape of the animals with their horns protruding out from the rope. Around them were bones of animals strewn everywhere.

I went into the field and started to untie the animals when someone yelled at me.

"DON'T DO THAT!"

I looked around and it was the man with the vest and the hat. Then I looked in the next field and saw a lot of buffalo penned up. They also were wrapped in rope so that only their horns protruded. I went over to the gate of that field and tried to break the lock to let them out.

The man in the vest and hat ran over and started reaching for me from the other side of the gate trying to stop me. As he clawed at me his hand was like a long knife. He started to scratch at me and I awoke with a yell.

As I sat there, wide awake, I tried to make sense of the dream. I was not one that found great meaning in dreams at that time but this one really grabbed me. Some psychiatrist could really have a good time with this one, I thought.

Was this something about my failing marriage? I had dreams about that and this was not the same. I sensed that it had to do with learning about native people, but then, I was no interpreter of dreams."

Misho nodded; "Some things are shown to us that reveal the truth in time. Spirit knows what we need in order to walk our walk."

CHAPTER THREE

Signs Begin to Appear

~ *Dbaad end'zin* ~ **[humility]** Humility to know that you are equal to everyone else. Take pride in what you do, but the pride that you take is in the sharing of the accomplishment with others.

The predicted snow storm was right on time. Snow started to come down lightly as the car crossed into Massachusetts. Soon it was coming down hard and the traffic began to slow on I-495 traveling around Boston. Cars and trucks were sliding around all over the place yet the Jeep just kept moving along as if it were on dry road.

Noodin told Misho of a time in the spring when he took his family camping, the family now being Noodin's son Nick, daughter Stephanie and himself. Monica never could seem to find the time anymore to join in on these outings. During the summer months Noodin would always take the kids camping as much as possible. They would start camping at Pillsbury State Park near Mt. Sunapee in New Hampshire. It is a great park for camping.

Misho; "My son mentioned that place to me the other day. Said he had been there with you awhile back."

"Nish Nung and I camped up there last summer, Misho." Noodin answered. "The park is considered primitive in that it does not have showers, electric and sewage hookups. It is a camping place for people who like quiet camping out where nature is close. The kids and I like to start our camping season there because there are several ponds nestled in the valleys and the wild life there is interesting. We particularly like that the Loons come in to nest in the spring and there are always at least two or three families of Loons living on those ponds. It is also a great place to hike and canoe. Lake Sunapee State Park is close by for swimming and that park has showers so we can clean up after being in the woods.

This camping trip had become our traditional annual breakdown trip. Bringing out all of our gear and checking out the equipment, making a list of things that we would need to camp through the summer and things that we would have to replace.

We found a good campsite and set up our tents and cooking gear. Nick and Steph went out to find sticks to start our fire while I put charcoal in our grill to cook dinner. We always eat well when we camp and I always start off by making a pot of coffee for myself and anyone that might stop by. The park ranger, Mike, knew us well and would always come up after dinner to say hello and have a cup of coffee.

Sure enough, after dinner Mike walked into our site and greeted the kids. I would usually read a story to the kids after dinner, before they would go to bed. On this trip I had forgotten the books that they enjoyed and the only book I had was "Bury My Heart at Wounded Knee". It was not really a book that I thought would be appropriate for a seven and eight year old but it is all I had with me. I had put the book on the table and during dinner I told the kids a little about it to see if they would be interested. Steph was okay with it and Nick thought a good Indian story would be great.

Mike noticed the book on the table as he sat down.

"Are you interested in Native American things?" Mike asked.

"Well, yes, a little." I answered and explained to him, somewhat apologetically, that the book would be our reading that night.

Mike suggested that there was to be a powwow down in Keene the next day.

"I hear it is really pretty good and you might want to take the kids there to see what it is about", he said.

"Well maybe", I said. "I didn't bring very much money so I don't know. We kind of were just planning to go hiking."

Mike went on; "I don't think it costs much from what I hear, you might want to try it."

Nick and Steph were already there in their heads. "Let's go there Dad, it might be fun," they said.

In the morning we made breakfast and put things away around our camp. It takes about an hour to get to Keene and we found the fairgrounds where the powwow was with no trouble. We went to the entry gate, $3 for me and $1 each for the kids, not bad.

As we walked up the path we saw a small crowd gathered around a lady under some birch trees. She was dressed in a beautiful white buckskin dress that was modestly beaded around the collar. Her hair was black with streaks of white showing her age and it hung nicely braided all the way down her back. On her left hand she wore a thick glove and on the glove stood perched, a large horned owl that looked out at the people. Behind her were all kinds of birds. There were hawks, other owls and even a golden eagle. That was as far as Steph wanted to go. She would have stayed there all day to be with those great birds.

It was Nick who started us off up the path again. A little further up the path was a wigwam that was cut half open so you could see in. That is what had caught Nick's eye. You could see pelts laid over the ground, carpeting the floor of the wigwam. On the inside hung different tools and weapons that were used by the Woodland Indians. Around the outside were more tools and a large turtle shell.

That is probably where I received my first oral teaching. Against the lodge was that huge turtle shell.

Nick asked me, "what did they use that shell for Dad?"

I asked the Indian standing next to the lodge. He told us that he is Micmac[11] and that the camp is a replica of how they lived hundreds of years ago.

"Many of the things here have been in my family for many generations", he added. "The turtle shell was used for many things. It could be used to carry water, to cook in, to store food, for a pouch to gather things and endless other uses."

The Indian asked; "How many full moons are there in a year?" I answered that there are twelve and he informed me that there are thirteen. Then he pointed to the shell and added, there are also thirteen

---

[11] Micmac in English, but Mi'kmaq (singular Mi'kmaw) by the Míkmaq of Nova Scotia, Miigmaq (Miigmao) by the Míkmaq of New Brunswick, Mi'gmaq by the Listuguj Council in Quebec, or Mìgmaq (Mìgmaw) in some native literature,[1] are a First Nations (Native American) people, indigenous to northeastern New England, Canada's Atlantic Provinces, and the Gaspé Peninsula of Quebec.

plates on the turtle shell. We are standing on turtle island, North America & South America. The earth is our mother and the moon is grandmother. Turtle offered himself to carry this land so that people would have a place to live. "These things are related." he said and continued; "Scientists recently concluded that the first life on land probably was carried onto land by the turtle. We could have told them that a long time ago, but they did not ask."

Then we heard the announcer at the powwow dance area announce that the grand entry was about to begin. We left the wigwam and followed the path to the powwow grounds.

The powwow grounds were large. A lot of people were walking around in native regalia we called costumes until we were abruptly corrected by an Indian that over heard us talking.

"We call the clothing we wear regalia." The Indian said rather sternly. "We are not wearing costumes. These things that we wear are traditionally what were worn by our ancestors. Each item has teachings and most of the clothing was hand made by the individual or by someone who made the item to gift to them. The clothing we wear is very personal and has great meaning to us. Please do not refer to the clothing as a costume". Without further adieu he walked away.

Most of the people did not look like Indians to me. They looked like white people in Indian regalia. Some had red or blond hair and they sometimes were wearing glasses and were white skinned. There were many who did look like Indians but then, I didn't really know what an Indian looked like anyhow except what I had seen in books and on TV or at the movies, and who knew how real they might be. Actually I didn't think there were any Indians around here anymore. The Indian regalia were varied in material and design.

The women usually wore long buckskin dresses. Some were plain in design while others had elaborate beading work. They often carried blankets or shawls neatly folded over one arm or draped over their shoulders and sometimes had a feather fan in the other hand. Some wore strange capes or had feathers for decoration in their hair. Many of the men also wore buckskin clothing. Again, some of it was very elaborate with beading all over. Others just wore a buckskin loincloth and were painted with different designs on their body. The dark skinned men dressed this way really looked very handsome but the white men looked kind of naked.

There was a large circle area roped off in the middle of the grounds with a fire going in the center. At the end was an arbor to protect the drummers from the heat of the sun. There was also an elaborate speaker system under the arbor that kind of took away from the realism a little. Outside the dance area were trader stalls under canvas cover that circled around the dance area. The traders had all sorts of things that were either Native American made or represented Native American. There were all kinds of clothing, blankets, flutes, drums, shakers, pelts, beads, buckskin and rawhide. Pelts of different animals hung from the stalls for sale for just two or three dollars.

The announcer again announced the Grand Entry and that the people should form up. Steph didn't want to leave the trader stalls and was totally taken with all these strange items for sale.

We walked over to the circle and stood there with all of the other tourists watching the gathering.

The announcer continued:" We are ready to begin. Welcome! The dancers will line up at the entry gate of the circle on the east end of the dance circle. Please line up behind the color guard, the Veterans first and then eldest men, then younger men. After the men the women will line up eldest to youngest and then the children.

The first song will be the entry song. If you are not wearing feathers, please remove your hats and all should stand through the grand entry, national anthem and veterans honor dance.

Oh yes, he added, please, no pictures should be taken at this time."

As he closed his introduction the drum sounded four times and then picked up a steady beat of the five drummers in unison. As the lead drummer began to sing, the Color Guard started to dance through the gate into the circle.

First to dance in was a Veteran dancer, then dancers carrying the American Flag, the American Indian Flag, the MIA flag, the Abenaki Flag, the Penobscot Flag, and the Iroquois Confederacy Flag and last another Veteran dancer. After the Color Guard came all of the people. The eldest of them often wore headdresses, to acknowledge that they were chiefs, I figured. The people all danced solemnly around the circle behind the Color Guard.

One young dancer with a beautiful buckskin set of clothes and a feather fan attached to his back, danced in front of the chiefs doing all kinds of beautiful steps.

When the song ended, the Color Guard was lined up facing the arbor where the drum was and the drum started again. All of the people dancing in the circle were lined up around the inside edge of the rope that made the circle for the dance area. They began to sing with the drum in a strange language that almost didn't sound like words, to me. The sound of the language was very foreign, like something I had never heard before. It was a beautiful song and almost felt timeless to hear. When that song ended the Colors were taken to the edge of the circle and posted.

The announcer then spoke: "The next dance will be the Veterans' song to honor all Veterans. If you are a Veteran of any service, the fire department, police or medical service also, please enter through the gate at the east end of the dance circle and join us. This song is to honor you."

WOW! I thought. They honor the Veteran. I had not admitted to being a Veteran for a long time after the welcoming home I got when I came out of service in 1967.

I was discharged at the time of Vietnam and the protest against the war was heated. Police were posted to accompany Vets for our protection when we would go to school on college campuses.

A girl at my work place found out I was a Veteran and attacked me at work. She asked me if I was a Vet. When I answered she started crying and hitting me on the chest calling me a baby killer. Another worker who was a Korean Veteran had to pull her off me. I never got over that and never admitted to being a Veteran after that.

Several people entered the circle and danced with the people that were Veterans. It made me feel proud that somebody actually cared about the Veterans. I had a very warm feeling for these people as they danced to that song. When that song ended most of the people left the circle.

Misho; "You were not proud to be a Veteran Noodin?"

"Vets were not well received when I came home from service in 1967, Misho. With the Vietnam War going on our welcome home was more a rejection by most people rather than a "welcome and we are proud of you".

"Yes, I remember those times. It is sad when people do not honor their warriors. The warrior is a protector of the people. People should understand that." Misho commented.

"What came next at the powwow?" Misho asked.

The announcer spoke again. "This dance will be inter-tribal. Everyone join us. It does not matter if you are Abenaki, Sioux, Apache or English or French. Come and join us for this dance."

I wanted to dance. The drum made me feel a deep urge to go out there but Nick and Steph said they didn't want to do it. I think they were afraid of looking silly. We watched the dancers for a long time. One song after another followed. Sometimes it seemed the singers were just chanting and other times it sounded like words of their Indian language, whatever that was.

The announcer came on again: "This song is for the children, the candy dance. All of you children come on in and dance. Adults, you can dance with them but only the children should collect candy. When the drum is going everyone dance and when the drum stops you grab all the candy you can find. When the drum starts again put down the candy you picked up and when it stops again you pick up more. Come on, all you kids and children at heart; join us in the dance circle."

I tried to get Steph and Nick to go in. "No way!" said Nick, but Steph said she would try it if I would go with her. We entered the circle and after a few steps to the beat of the drum we were dancing. An Indian, all painted and dressed in an animal skin, danced up behind us and let out a loud shrill war hoop. I don't know who jumped higher, Steph or me; we both laughed and kept dancing. It was great fun for both of us but all the coaxing in the world was not going to get Nick to join us. We left late in the afternoon after having had a wonderful day at a powwow.

That night we sat by our fire and Mike stopped in. He had finished his rounds and came by with his two daughters and joined us. Steph was always happy when Mike would bring his kids along so that she would have someone to play with. Play with her brother was more like an ongoing war.

"So how was the powwow?" Mike asked.

"It was great, Mike. Thank you for suggesting it. We learned a lot. I didn't even know Indians did that sort of thing anymore. We were talking at dinner, the kids and I, and we are thinking we will spend our camping time this summer checking out Indian history around New England; see what we can learn sort of thing." I answered.

Mike replied that it sounded like a good idea and gave me a few suggestions of books that I might want to get that would point us in the right direction. In winter Mike is a science and history teacher in Peterborough so he is aware of a lot of the history of the area.

I asked Mike what he had done all day.

He told us; "I have a good crew on this year so after I gave them their work assignments I went out to gather water samples."

"What are the water samples for?" I asked.

"These ponds were part of a stream and the dam at the south end of them was created to fill the pond areas. Mike answered. "They used these ponds to float logs down to where they could take them by road when they were timbering this area back around the turn of the twentieth century. I have pictures of some of the buildings that were here then. They are back at the office. You can look at them when you come down if you want. They used to mark the logs with mercury marks [12] and that mercury has built up in the mud in the bottom of the lakes. That pollutes the water, the fish and everything downstream. I gather samples and send it into the State so they can monitor the level of mercury in the water."

"Is it very bad?" I asked.

"I wouldn't eat any fish out these ponds." he answered, "Though a lot of people do. The cleanest pond is up near the mountain but they are progressively more polluted as you get down to the lower areas. It will be a long time before the ponds are clean again because that mercury is settled in the muck at the bottom."

"Another contribution of modern civilization I suppose." I said.

"Yes!" He replied. "When you are out here working in the woods you begin to see the damage caused that most people don't know anything about."

Mike and his kids left and we turned in for the night.

Through the summer we camped in Vermont, Maine and Massachusetts as well as our usual haunts in New Hampshire. Every weekend we would go someplace different and we would visit places that had any history to tell us more about the people that had lived on this land for thousands of years. There were sites dating back as far as nine thousand years."

"It is good that you care for your family, Noodin." Misho commented.

Misho went on, "In the early 1900's my grandfather was invited to visit St. Paul / Minneapolis by the Governor and some politicians. They wanted to show the Indians the progress made in the cities that were forming. The politicians took them around to all of the buildings made of stone and the parks that had been made here and there. They showed them the power plant and the factories being powered by the water of the three rivers that flow through the cities. When they had completed their tour the politicians asked my grandfather what he thought of all of this. His answer has come to be what is: "There will come a day when we have to pay for the water we drink!"

---

[12] Concern over the potential health hazards of mercury levels in fish led the United States Food and Drug Administration (FDA) and the Environmental Protection Agency (EPA) to issue consumption guidelines in March 2004.

CHAPTER FOUR

Man or Spirit

~**Maiingun**~ [wolf] Wolf is brother in spirit to man. Wolf is matter of fact in his effort to look after his family. His humility lies in being himself.

The roads were now covered with two or three inches of snow. Considering the weather, they were still making good time traveling toward Rochester, New Hampshire. The traffic disappeared as cars pulled off the road to escape from the storm. It was an easy ride as long as they were alert and careful. Telling Misho about these things helped to keep Noodin in an alert state for the long drive.

To Noodin it was a beautiful time to travel. The storm reduced traffic and the snow is so beautiful to see coming down and toward the lights of the car as it moves down the road.

"The summer, Misho, had been an adventure of seeing and doing new things for the family and me. Most of all it brought an awareness of the people that lived here for thousands of years. At the end of the summer it had become a family tradition for us to take one long trip for ten days or more and go someplace special. The whole family together, well, this year Monica would not be joining us, but Nick, Steph and I would make a trip. I suggested that we go to Alleghany State Park in Western New York. I had never visited there and had grown up in Western New York. We could visit the Salamanca Seneca Reservation[13] and I would be able to take the kids to some of the places I used to go to with my parents and friends including Lake Cayuga, Lake Genesee and Letch worth State Park.

I was born in Western New York in the heart of the Iroquois[14] Seneca land. It made sense to me to learn about the beliefs of these people who had lived for at least a thousand years in the place where I had been born.

I wanted to do something special to wind up our search for the Indians through the summer. I had an idea! My mind kept going back to that book, "Bury My Heart at Wounded Knee". The spiritual aspect of survival that the Indian people had so magnificently demonstrated kept nagging at my thoughts. That Spirit understanding that seemingly had gone unnoticed by history. What would an Indian Elder say about that I wondered? I had an idea.

I didn't tell the kids but I called the Seneca Reservation Council in Salamanca. There was no answer to their phones, just a "please leave a message" response. Then, I called the Bureau of Indian Affairs in Washington. I told the lady who answered I wanted to see if an Elder of the Seneca people would be willing to talk to my children and share a little about the Indian culture. She replied that she doubted I would find someone but that I could call the Salamanca Indian Library and she gave me a number. When I called the library, a

---

[13] The Seneca Nation of Indians (SNI) is one of the six tribes of the Iroquois Confederacy who occupy aboriginal lands in New York State set aside by the Treaty of Canandaigua of 1794. The Seneca Nation of Indians has a total population of over 7200 enrolled members and holds title to three territories in New York, one of which includes the City of Salamanca.

[14] The Iroquois Confederacy or Haudenosaunee (also known as the "League of Peace and Power", the "Five Nations"; the "Six Nations"; or the "People of the Longhouse") is a group of First Nations/Native Americans that originally consisted of five nations: the Mohawk, the Oneida, the Onondaga, the Cayuga, and the Seneca. A sixth tribe, the Tuscarora, joined after the original five nations were formed. When Europeans first arrived in North America, the Confederacy was based in what is now the northeastern United States primarily in what is referred to today as Upstate New York.

woman answered; "Salamanca Indian Library, I am Elma, may I help you?"

I explained who I am and that I wanted my children to understand the Native American people.

"We are going to go camping at Alleghany State Park in two weeks." I said. "We would like to sit down with an Elder and to have that Elder tell us a little about the Seneca people."

"We don't do that!" she said. "I don't think anyone has asked us to do that before. I will ask around and when you get here stop at the library. Ask for Elma and I will let you know if I can find anyone."

"Thank you Elma, I really appreciate it," I answered as politely as I could.

"Two weeks later Nick, Steph and I packed all of our gear in the car and loaded on the canoe. We were off for the nine hour drive to Alleghany State Park in Western New York. We were set for ten days of exploration and adventure in the great outdoors. All day we drove through the beautiful valleys of New York and wondered at the beauty as we traveled. The winds were strong that day and we could feel the wind grabbing at the canoe as we traveled, trying to pull our car from side to side. When we arrived in Salamanca we headed straight for the park and drove five miles in to camp area #3 where we would make camp. I had reserved our site in advance so that we would be sure to have a place to camp. The kids set up their tent and went out to explore while I put up my tent and set up the rest of our camp. That night was pleasant and reasonably quiet considering there were 250 other campsites in that area. Sitting by the fire, we planned the day to come. It was supposed to rain all day so it would be a good day to go down and explore Salamanca. We would see the Indian Museum, check out the stores, pick up some supplies and, oh yes, we could stop at the Indian library. I still had not told the kids about my query to find an Elder. I wasn't too hopeful anyhow after talking to the woman at the library. She did not seem too anxious to help me find an Elder. I went to sleep that night listening to the crackling of my fire and a low murmur of voices coming from the camp next to us. At least they were being respectful and talking in low voices, I thought as I dozed off.

The morning was cloudy and damp and I awoke late. Probably tired from the drive the day before, I thought. I generally wake up right at daylight when we camp. I started some coffee on my stove and built a small fire to take away the chill of the mountain air. We would have pancakes and bacon for breakfast so I began to get that ready. The clouds were really dark in the west so if we wanted breakfast without getting soaked we would have to hurry. It would be a good day to go to town rather than stay there in the rain. The kids got up and I rushed them a little so we could eat before the rain came. We finished breakfast and picked up the camp just as the first drops began. By the time we got in the car it was a downpour and it would last all day. The drive to town was beautiful. Everything was lush green and the rain made it look like everything was in a big shower, glistening with the cleansing water of the downpour.

We found the Indian museum and ran inside to try to stay dry. Fat chance, it was pouring harder each hour. It is a great museum and very informative about the history of the Seneca people. They had scenic displays with stuffed animals and canoes beached on streams, explanation of the wampum for money, treaty and trade, a copy of the entire Great Law, Regalia and scenes of people living daily lives amongst the Seneca. By the time we completed our tour the rain had let up a little. We went down town to see what this town was like. It is the only incorporated city within the border of an Indian reservation in the United States. It is a good size town but the downtown area was more like a ghost town. Most of the stores were boarded up and some were in major disrepair. Not much to impress. It kind of reminded me of all of those towns in the mid west along old route 40 just off the Interstate. Those towns had bustling businesses as farm towns in the first half of the twentieth century. They basically became like ghost towns when the interstate came to be in the fifties and sixties. Salamanca is like that. We stopped at one store where we could get some supplies and the kids picked up a few trinkets to remember the trip and something for Mom.

Now it was raining hard again so I suggested that we visit the library. Nick and Steph said fine, though I could tell that they did not think this was a great place to go while on a vacation.

If you ever want to find a book about Indians you would want to visit this library. I had no idea that there could be so many books written about Native American people. While the kids looked around I went up to the desk.

A young Indian woman looked up and said, "Yes, can I help you?"

I told her; "My name is Jim Beard and I am looking for Elma".

"I am Elma." She replied. "Oh yes, you called here a few weeks ago didn't you."

"Yes", I replied.

She indicated that she had asked around but no one seemed able to help. "I don't know anyone that will talk with you", she said, "but I will check one more place. Come by tomorrow and I will let you know. Where are you staying while you are here?" she asked.

"We are camped up in the park at camp area #3." I answered.

"Like I said, I don't think there is anyone who will help you with this." She added, "But come by anyway." She was very nice but I could tell that she wasn't really too comfortable with my inquiry.

It was just as I thought. It was foolish of me to think I could just walk in and some great Elder would suddenly appear to share with me all the knowledge they have so carefully protected through the years.

The rain was coming down in torrents so we found a little restaurant in town for dinner and took our time going back to camp. The rain let up when we returned and everything had remained dry in the tents.

I made a fire and the kids went to sleep early. I sat by the fire and looked at the stars beginning to appear in the sky. It looked like it was going to be a beautiful night and the stars seemed somehow bigger here than at home. The forest had a fresh moist smell that drifted through in a light breeze and mixed with the smoke from the fire. It had been a good day and hopefully, the weather would clear so we could spend more time outdoors. I went to sleep thinking about how nice it was here in the park with no daily pressures and nature all around.

It was still dark out. I thought I heard something outside my tent and awoke with a start. What was that I wondered? Then I heard a crackling of a fire and saw light on the side of my tent. The crackling was close. That is my fire! I had put it out last night so how could it have started up with no wood. I heard someone pick up a piece of kindling and put it into the fire. It couldn't be the kids?!

"This is my camp!" I said, in as strong and firm a voice as I could muster. "Can I help you?" I tensely waited for a response.

A quiet, yet also strong, male voice came back. "Are you looking for someone to tell you about the Iroquois people?"

"Yes I am." I answered.

"Why don't you come out and we can talk?" Said the voice from outside my tent.

I quickly put on my pants and shirt, thinking to myself, this can't really be happening. Who is this guy and what have I gotten myself into this time?

As I came out of my tent I looked up at the man standing on the other side of the fire. He was tall, about 6'2" and had a strong solid looking build. His hair was black with gray streaks and hung loosely over his shoulders and down his back. Even with the gray in his hair he didn't look much older than his mid forties. His jeans were weathered and he wore an old sweatshirt with a faded picture of whales on it. The features of his face were unmistakably Indian and he had a proud and contented look about him. He looked to have a quiet and gentle demeanor and to be very much at peace with himself.

"I knew you were coming." he said. "I had a dream two weeks ago that you and your children would be here and would camp in this place."

I was taken back a little. How could this man find us out here? I thought, what did he mean, he knew we were coming?

"I brought coffee," he continued, and handed me a cup of Dunkin Donuts coffee. The coffee was hot, fresh and strong. No sugar added. It was just the way I like it.

I went over to my car and took out a red wrap of tobacco to give him. I wanted him to see that I was aware of the customs of the Native people.

"I brought tobacco." I said, and handed a cloth wrap of tobacco to him.

He took it and said; "I know."

What is this? I thought. This isn't believable.

He invited me to sit down and he sat on the other side of the fire. He put a donut bag down beside him, and said, "My name is Maize and I am from the Cattaraugus Reservation over by Lake Erie."

He looked up at me and straight into my eyes, yet somehow deeper. "Why do you ask about us?" He said.

I thought to myself; well that is cutting to the quick of it.

I answered; "I want my children to know the truth about Native American people."

He didn't say anything for a moment and looked back at the fire. Then he slowly looked up, looking me straight in the eyes again, and asked more slowly; "Why do you ask about us?"

I told him that I want to understand spirit teachings of the people. What I have found about my own ancestors doesn't give me what I am seeking and I am looking to the Indian to see if what I seek is there.

Now I had said it! I am seeking an understanding of the spirit teachings of the Indian. I have felt drawn in this direction as I have become aware of the Indian over the past year or so.

He answered; "There are those who are Indian in heart, which must be why I heard you. I will talk to you and your children. Wake them and ask them to join us. I brought donuts for them. I will smoke this tobacco you gave me tonight when I get home."

The kids got up and came out. They were already dressed when I went to get them and had been listening to Maize and I talking.

I introduced the kids; "This is Stephanie, my daughter and Nick, my son and kids, this is Maize. He has come by to talk to us about the Seneca people."

Nick and Steph courteously said hello and sat down by the fire.

Maize began; "We Seneca are a proud people and have lived here for thousands of years. Our people were at odds with each other for a long time. There were wars between the Iroquois tribes and among each other in our bands and amongst our clans. It was a bad time and only looked as if it would get worse. That is when Deganawida[15] came to us from the west of the great lake in a stone canoe. He brought teachings that could help us to live peacefully with each other. He met Hyonwada [Hi-on-wa-ta / Hiawatha], a chief of the Seneca and they traveled throughout the Iroquois tribes speaking the words of what we call the Great Law. Five of our nations gathered together and formed a Confederacy to live by the Great Law. Our nations are formed under the great white tree of Creator and we buried our weapons of destruction we had used on each other. The Seneca, Oneida, Onondaga, Cayuga and Mohawk became the five nations of the Confederacy. Later, the Tuscarora Nation would join the confederacy and it would become six nations as it is today. We are our own country and the only other countries that do not recognize us as a sovereign nation are the United States and Canada. We have a seat at the Geneva Convention and our own passports and licenses.

Our Confederacy lived in peace for a long time until the white man came. When they had their wars, our people were divided. Some fought for the British and some for the French. Later in the revolution some were loyal to the British and others supported the colonists. The Seneca even took corn to Washington's troops in the winter when they were starving. The split of our people nearly destroyed our Confederacy but we came back. Our people thought Washington would kill our people after the revolution and many went to Canada to

---

[15] Deganawida or The Great Peacemaker, the traditional founder along with Hiawatha of the Haudenosaunee Confederacy.

get away. Washington forgave the people that sided against him and for that reason we think he is the only white man that will go to heaven.

We have Clans that our people belong to. If a man wants to marry a woman she must be of another Clan. When he marries he will go to live with her people and become a part of her clan. The Clan Mother and the women select our leaders and put the one selected up before the tribe to be accepted as leaders. The Clan women can also demote a leader who they do not favor. The Clan is everything to the people. The woman is seen as the most important of the people because she is "at one" with Mother Earth and the bearer of the children. If you kids were misbehaving your mother would throw you in the river so you would behave."

Nick and Steph smiled as Maize laughed.

Maize continued, "We have councils that are part of our medicine societies. There are several medicine societies; the mask society, the long house society and others. The understanding we have with Creator and all of our relations are the basis of our lives. Only a few of us still follow our old ways. Many are now Christians and many more don't follow much of anything. That is why we have so many bad things happening to our people.

Life here in Salamanca is difficult for our people. The white people dominate our schools and businesses. I have a nephew who went to kindergarten here. Some white kids made fun of him and pushed him down a stairs. Now he has a cleft lip and will never be the same. If Indians had done that they would have been punished but nothing was done to the white kids. We don't get involved in sports here because the white kids dominate the sports.

Many of our people commit suicide, many more than in a normal population. Diabetes, cancer and heart disease are higher amongst us as well. A lot of our children quit school as soon as they can and hang out down town smoking and drugging. A lot of our people are in jail."

It was about eleven in the morning and Maize got up and said, "I gotta go now but I will be back tomorrow." He turned and walked up the road toward the camp entry gate without another word.

"We will see you then." I hollered after him.

The kids and I put things away and decided to take a ride to see the old Quaker settlement in the south end of the park. It began raining again and we found a little museum in the Quaker area. We went in and spent time looking at different furniture and paintings. The history said that the

Quakers were always on good terms with the Iroquois and served as missionaries to them. They also argued for protection for the Indians in the Continental Congress. We looked at the homes where Quakers had lived. It was a beautiful hill country. Very quiet and serene.

As it began to clear in the later afternoon we decided to take the opportunity to go for a canoe ride on a small lake and have a swim. That night we hiked around trails near our camp and looked at the different flowers and scenery in the area. When we got back to the camp, the kids went down to a stream behind our camp and played with other kids in the water. I cooked dinner.

The next morning I got up at sunrise and set our fire. When I turned around from lighting the fire, Maize was standing there behind me.

"You have a long walk ahead of you." he said matter of factly.

"I do? What do you mean?" I replied.

He answered, "You will find out. I can see that you have a long walk. That is all!"

We sat and drank coffee for a long time. He told me that he gets up early. "Don't sleep much. " He added.

"What do you do for work?" I asked.

"I work at different things." He answered. "In the morning I smoke my pipe before I do anything and again at night before I sleep. I do that every day. My path is with Spirit every day, not just Sunday. That is what gives me a good life. Most of my brothers still suffer but I know the old ways can make me a better man. You will see! The spirit world is right here with us. Most people don't see it, or don't pay attention when they do. You learn the teachings and then you start to see it. After a time you begin to notice the signs. Then you begin to know how to see the signs and understand them. Like I said, it is a long walk. You already have all the answers, you just don't know it."

It is about eight thirty by now so I woke up the kids. "Breakfast will be ready in a couple of minutes, kids." I started some pancakes and bacon in a pan. I offered Maize some but he wouldn't eat. He just sat quietly and drank coffee until we had finished.

Maize told the kids about the Allegheny reservoir[16] and how it came to be. "We tried to stop the reservoir." he said. "A lot of our homes were located on the river where the reservoir was to be built.

---

[16] In 1964, amid controversy, anger, and the protests of many Seneca Indians, ... from an Indian cemetery ("our Arlington," pleaded a Seneca woman) that was about to be ... Behind the dam is the new Allegheny Reservoir.

We could not see what good would come of moving us and building a reservoir. The government would not listen to our protests. They built us new housing away from the river and on a hill. Our people had lived in a village in that place along the river for as long as anyone could remember. The government didn't care that it is our land under treaty or that we wanted to stay there on the river. We set up barricades and tried to stop them. Even went to court but nothing worked to stop those people. They built the dam and filled the reservoir. When it was all over the engineers discovered that they did not need a reservoir there anyhow."

"But the Indians got new homes," said Nick.

"Yes, we got new homes, but at what cost? We lost our ancestral homes and all of the land that belonged to us that is now under water. It was just one more way the government could take something away. They do it all the time."

"Even now?" Nick asked.

"Yes, even now." Maize answered. "A few years ago the government decided to restrict our tobacco allotments because people were coming to the reservation to buy cigarettes that are not taxed. We stood by our right to do with our tobacco what we wanted."

"Maize.", I said, "The kids don't know anything about tobacco and the Indians."

"Yes I do." Nick responded. "The Indians would raise tobacco and showed the colonists how to grow it and smoke it. That is why everybody started smoking."

Maize continued: "Tobacco is a Sacred Medicine we use to offer prayers to Creator. Smoking like people do today is abusing this medicine. We smokers, your Dad and me included, know that it is a bad way to use the tobacco. When we smoke that way we know it may make the medicine work against us and can make us sick. We make choices and with tobacco, people sometimes choose to abuse it.

The government action though, was a clear violation of our treaties. Many highways cross over our reservations like the New York State Throughway in Oneida, New York and Tonawanda New York. To stop the government, our people in Oneida blocked the Throughway there. That effectively closed down a main artery through New York State and we got attention."

"I remember that," I said. "I was in high school when that happened."

Maize went on; "After a short time the government threatened to bring in armed troops to remove the Indians from the blockade and arrest them. The government said that the blockade was interfering with the U.S. Mail by stopping the flow of traffic. That ended the blockade but the government also backed down on the restriction of our tobacco allotment and our right to do with it what we want. There are many examples of these things just among the Iroquois Confederacy and many more in other nations of the people across the country."

Maize then stood up. "I gotta go now." He said. "I'll be back tomorrow." He then turned and walked up the road.

It was eleven thirty in the morning and we visited a rock formation in the park. It is a great accumulation of sandstone that has been smoothed and washed over thousands of years and stands near the top of a hill in the park. It looks like a sculpture with rounded curves and holes in and around the stone. The kids had a great time climbing and running in and around the stone. We did not realize that there might be any danger until that night when we got back to camp. The ranger in the park told us to be careful around there because the rocks are infested with rattlesnakes. Great to know after the fact! We had a swim that evening and then settled in at camp for the night.

Somebody dropped an armload of firewood outside my tent. I knew it must be Maize and I got up and put on some coffee while Maize built a fire. He didn't say anything as he started the fire. He just sat down and watched the fire build up. I noticed that he always field stripped his cigarettes and put the filter in his pocket. I would put the spent cigarette in the fire. Actually, I put a lot of things into the fire. It was a good way to keep the accumulation of trash down.

"Why do you strip your cigarettes instead of putting them into the fire?" I asked.

Maize looked up slowly and with a solemn look that emphasized the seriousness of what he would say. The fire lit up his face and the high cheekbone features so common to his ancestry made him look timeless, as he began to speak.

"The fire is sacred." He answered. "It is the responsibility of man to care for the fire, just as it is the responsibility of woman to care for the water. We need to respect these things. He looked down at the fire. There was a time when all fires burned a color of blue. It was a time when all things were in balance long ago. It is said that, if we as a people, can come back to balance, the fires will burn blue once again. I have seen blue fires when the people are being respectful. Only proper offerings should be put into a fire and those should be offered respectfully."

Maize then said; "Wake up the kids. There is a place I want to show to all of you."

I woke the kids and told them to get ready for a hike. They were glad to be going for a walk in the woods. It is one of their favorite things to do.

Maize led the way down and across the stream behind our camp. We continued straight over the road and into the woods. No path to follow, just straight into the woods. After a short time we saw some deer run off ahead of us.

Steph said, "I like seeing the wildlife."

Nick, who saw them first, said we would see them again.

Maize commented; "You are right Nick, we will!"

We came to a place near a stone outcropping and Maize stopped. He was very still and quiet and then pointed to the top of a tree. A huge hawk was sitting in the very top of the tree looking down at us. "Hawk is watching our trail," Maize said.

After walking a little further into a grove of pine trees Maize stopped again. He pointed at some droppings under the trunk of a large pine tree. "Owl is keeping watch from here." He said. We looked up and sure enough, half way up the tree sat perched, a large Barred Owl.

We kept hiking and saw more and more animals. There were black squirrels, a porcupine, blue jays, woodpeckers and lots of small birds. It seemed as if all the animals came out that morning. We walked across a trail but Maize stayed to the woods and continually traveled up hill. It almost was as if the woods opened up in a straight line to let us pass. All the time we were going uphill, but it did not seem like anything more than a walk on flat land. Maize seemed to know exactly where he wanted to take us. As we walked Maize would point to different plants and trees. We use the root of this plant for medicine. This fern is a woman's medicine and those mushrooms are the best for flavor in a stew. We came to a roaring stream and Maize brought us out at the exact place where the stream narrowed enough for us to cross it. The forest was a lush green and had a pleasant moist smell that you rarely would notice except after a good hard rain. Everything seemed so alive with animals running here and there and birds singing and flying around us.

"Most forests aren't this healthy," Maize said. He pointed to the top of the trees and added; "Even this healthy forest is affected by man's pollution. The leaves of the higher parts of the trees were curled and had a tainted brown color to them. You can see the damage caused by acid rain. This affects everything in the forest. All of the plants, the animals and the earth, our mother."

Further up we came to a large open area covered with ledge rock. We kept climbing in a straight line and it was as if the ledge had somehow been cut in a way as to make a walk for us to continue on in that straight line. We went back into the forest for a short while and then into an open field at the top of a small mountain. When we reached the top it was an amazing scene to look out upon in every direction. You could see the Allegheny River meandering in from the east and winding around the north end of the hills and then turning to the southwest working its way into Pennsylvania. To the East and South we looked on rolling green mountains that gently rolled out, one after another with the backdrop of a blue sky filled with little cloud puffs. To the west was an open body of water, a long way off was Lake Erie. Other lakes and valleys dotted the landscape. What a beautiful place! What a magical place to look down from.

Maize commented after awhile: "This is a special place for my people. Not many come here anymore though. We should go now. The rain is coming."

I looked around and couldn't see anything but blue skies and a few clouds to the east. "Are you sure it is going to rain?" I asked.

Maize kind of glanced at me as if to say, you don't believe me?

"We have to go now," he said.

We went back down exactly the way we had come up the mountain. Maize seemed to know every part of the forest where we were traveling. As we progressed down the mountain we came upon another herd of deer grazing on the upper meadow.

"There sure are a lot of deer in these woods." Said Steph.

"Same ones." Maize said flatly.

When we got back to camp it was already four o'clock in the afternoon. It had seemed like a short walk but had taken most of the day. Maize took a swig of the cold coffee in the cup he had been drinking from that morning.

Maize said, "It is time for me to go. I will see you again."

He gave each of the kids a hug and then came over and gave me a hug.

"Don't give up!" He said.

"Maize, have you got a phone number and address so we can stay in touch?" I asked.

"I don't have a phone and I move around a lot. We will meet again." He answered.

He clasped my hand and reached out to give me a hug with his free arm.

Just as he was leaving it started to rain. We were really hungry and grilled up a good dinner. After that we drove down to the park center to get some ice cream.

Nick asked; "Will we see Maize again?"

"I don't know, I think that was his last visit." I answered.

Steph said, "I like him, he explains things good."

As we were leaving the area I decided to swing by the Library and thank them. Maybe we would have a chance run in with Maize or at least find out how to reach him. Elma was in her chair.

"I just came in to thank you, Elma, for your help." I told her.

"It was nothing", she replied. "I am sorry I could not find anyone for you."

I looked at her. We obviously weren't communicating. "I mean for sending Maize up to our camp to talk with us." I explained.

Now it was her turn to look at me funny.

"I didn't send anyone to talk to you." She said. "I couldn't find anyone."

"Yes, you must have. A man named Maize." I answered.

"I never heard of Maize and nobody told me they would talk to you and your kids." was her answer.

I responded; "You don't know Maize? He is tall and has a strong build. Long blackish gray hair that he lets hang down his back. He wears a T-shirt and Jeans."

"That could be a lot of people I know, but I never heard of Maize." Elma replied.

"Ok!" I said hesitantly. "Well thank you for your help anyhow."

Misho and Noodin were almost to Rochester now. Noodin looked over at Misho in the light from the streetlights and it looked as if there were tears in his eyes.

"Well Misho, during that summer I began to follow this path in earnest. I think, when Maize said to me, "You have a long way to go", I realized that my life had changed and that there are things that I must do."

Misho answered. "You have been on this path longer than you know Noodin. You will see. Maize knew that when he told you that you have a long walk ahead of you."

CHAPTER FIVE

To Find a Home

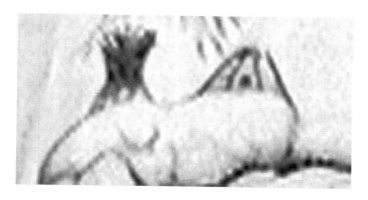

~ *Gwe kwaad ziwin* ~ **[honesty] Be** honest in every action and provide good feelings in the heart. Do not be deceitful or use self-deception.

Misho and Noodin arrived in Rochester about a half hour late due to the snowstorm. During the drive they hardly noticed the force of the storm. The nice thing about it is that there was hardly any traffic and the Jeep travels well in adverse weather.

"What are you going to talk about to these people?" Misho asked as they got out of the car.

"They have asked for information about the Medicine Wheel and Prophesy. I am going to tell them about the Seven Teachings first. Not sure how I am going to do that though."

"Just tell them the story", Misho said.

"The first Elder and the seven gifts?" Noodin answered.

"Yes. You know that story don't you?" Replied Misho.

"Yes, but I have never told it before", Noodin answered.

Chris was waiting at the door and came out to help Noodin bring in the projector and his things.

Chris is a quiet man about average height. He is a master in tai-chi martial arts and encourages his students to broaden their understanding of spirit in order to be complete in their practice of martial arts.

"Misho, this is Chris. He is the owner of this school. Chris, this is Misho. He is my teacher." Noodin said.

Chris and Misho greeted one another and talked for a moment while Noodin gathered his things.

The three men entered the building and greeted Chris's students. There were about eighteen people in all.

Misho took a chair and sat over to the side. Noodin introduced Misho as his Elder and informed the group that Misho would be joining them for the evening. Everyone was excited to have Misho as a guest and they all wanted to meet this man, this Indian Elder.

Noodin set up a projector and laid out some of his native bundle. On a blanket, he placed a shell filled with sage, a feather fan and a sign informing people that donations are acceptable along with a basket for donations.

Everyone took a place sitting on the floor and in chairs set up in a circle and Noodin began the presentation. He introduced Misho once again in a more formal manner and told them a little about himself before starting. During this introduction, Noodin asked Chris to take the lit sage and smudge the people with a feather fan, which he did.

The first part of the presentation was about Spirit and to present it Noodin told the legend of the Seven Gifts and the first Elder as Misho had suggested. Misho was very intent as he listened and Noodin felt nervous starting out. As he got into the legend he forgot about Misho being there and became absorbed in the telling of the story.

The second part of the program was on Prophesy so Noodin presented a comparison of eastern and western prophesy. He noted the European linear approach and its contrast to aboriginal prophesy that travels in a circle to regenerate. The end of a time is not the end; rather it is a change to another time.

The presentation took about two hours and everyone seemed to enjoy the program.

Misho talked with Chris while Noodin loaded up the car. The snow had stopped and the roads did not look too bad for the three hour ride back to Connecticut.

As they pulled out to the highway Noodin asked Misho what he thought.

"You present good. You have the legend down too. You left out the Otter helper spirit though and that is an important part of the legend. Sometimes, listening to you I could almost see the boy gathering his bundle," Misho answered.

The snow had stopped and it was late, around ten thirty, so there was no traffic to speak of. New Hampshire towns get real quiet later at night in general. The roads had cleared too so the drive was easy and relaxing as Noodin continued the conversation with Misho.

"I remember telling that legend in a circle a couple of years ago. You sounded a lot like me when you told it," Said Misho.

"When you told it a couple of years ago is when I heard the story," Noodin responded.

Misho asked; "how did you come to know the Ojibwe? How did you come to our circle?"

Noodin answered, "After that summer traveling with Nick and Steph, it seemed like all things came to a sudden halt with regard to all the native information that had been flowing so well. I thought of all the things that Maize had told the kids and me. About the powwows we went to and the people that we met. I was checking different web sites, thirsting for more information about the spiritual beliefs of the indigenous people of America.

Most of the winter was spent reading any books I could find about the Iroquois. I went to a couple of winter powwows to see if I could find someone to teach me, but to no avail. Even tried to find the man I met at Alleghany State Park, Tom Maize, but there was no information to be found on him. There is a Maize family on the Cattaraugus Reservation but they have no one named Tom in the family.

I focused on the Iroquois Confederacy and particularly on the Seneca Nation. I felt that it would be best to learn the teachings of a specific group of people rather than many groups in general. My initial experience had shown that most of the beliefs of indigenous people were different but came to similar conclusions and seemed somehow connected. The difference seemed more specifically to do with the ritual, legends and Geographic regions of the people. The Seneca were the people of the land where I was born and raised so it therefore made sense to me to learn from their customs, since I already had a little understanding of the geography and history of the area.

There is a lot about the Iroquois on the Internet. Some of it is from people who feel that we of European decent should go back to

Europe and leave them alone. Others seem anxious to help all people understand the history and language of the Native people. There is no end of political views about treaties, rights, sovereignty and casinos, as well as who took what from whom. Many concerns are about health and the drug and alcohol problems as well as the gambling addictions of the people. Many sites point to the language and the importance of retaining it among the younger of the people.

In all that I could find, there was little that was really helpful when it came to the Spirit teachings of the people. What little I could find seemed rather superficial in content and would hint at a vast knowledge that would not be revealed.

If only I could find an Elder! If I could spend more time with someone like Maize! It had become obvious to me that the Native American culture holds a belief system that mirrors what I believe. Maybe I am just too simple to understand the great wealth of factual information of the so called theologians of the world. I guess so."

"You were looking for an Iroquois elder then," Misho asked?

"Yes! At that time I was." Noodin answered.

"How do you find an Elder who will share with you the knowledge that they hold? If you go to a known Elder and ask a question, the answer you will inevitably hear is, "I don't know anything". Even native people in this day and age have difficulty in finding an elder. For a white man the odds seem insurmountable. The only thing for me to do would be to trust in my faith and learn what I can. I would ask Spirit that when a man of Elder status could see I am seeking truth in my heart with sincerity, then that elder might offer to help.

I kept reading what I could find and going to powwows around New England. I met people, some who claimed to be Elders. I would talk to them and realize that they did not know much more than I had found out on my own, if that. Others spoke about knowledge in such a way that I knew I did not want what they had.

I attended one powwow where I met a man who would affect my teachings. At a powwow in Warner NH at the Mt. Kearsage Indian Museum, I met a man named Barry White Crow Higgons. He seemed to be a gentle person with a sense of balance in his life.

When I first saw him he was doing a presentation about the Native American flute. He demonstrated the flute and told about how to make them. In his demonstration he told the story of how the flute came to the people. Then he performed with the flute. The music he played was unbelievable and calming beyond anything that I heard before.

I had purchased a flute a month or so before but felt at odds about making music with it. I certainly would never play it around a place where someone might hear my lame attempts.

When I saw him on the powwow grounds later I went up and introduced myself.

"Barry, my name is Jim and I really enjoyed hearing you perform. I wonder, could I ask you for some help?" I reached into my pocket and took out a tobacco wrap and offered it to him.

He looked at the tobacco wrap and said; "I am not an Elder!"

"To me you are since you hold knowledge that I do not have about the flute", I said.

"What can I help you with," he asked?

"I have a flute and I am trying to learn to play but I don't know how to do much with it," I answered.

"Do you have the flute with you?" Barry asked?

"Yes, it is in my car," I said.

Then he suggested; "Bring it here and we can check it out".

"Thank you, Barry," I answered.

I went to get my flute. This feels a little nerve racking to me I thought. He wants to look at the flute right there in the middle of a powwow.

I was impressed that he was so open to help and willing to give me a little time. A lot of people were coming up to him and he was obviously busy with the work he had come there to do as a performer.

"Here it is," I said, as I approached him.

He looked at the flute for a moment and then handed it back to me.

He looked at me and said; "Play it for me."

"Here? Now?" I replied.

"Yes!" he said. "Let me hear what it sounds like when you play."

I took a breath and began to play. A few squeaks here and missed notes there and I ploughed through a tune that kind of went up and down the scale. It sounded terrible to me and I really felt nervous as I ended.

Barry remarked; "You play pretty good for just starting out. That is a nice flute but I think it is out of tune a little. May I try it?"

I handed him my flute and he began to play. I suddenly heard my flute sing out beautiful notes and play music that was soothing and beautiful. I could not help but wonder that my flute could sound that good.

Barry said; "My Indian name is White Crow and I am Abenaki. I make flutes and do programs in schools to teach kids about the flute. If you would like, you could come to my home and I will make some changes that will tune this flute. It plays really well now but I can fix a couple of the notes for you."

"That would be great," I said.

White Crow gave me directions to his home.

Then White Crow asked, "Would you like to help me? I am going to do another presentation in a few minutes."

I answered; "Sure, what do you want me to do?"

Barry replied; "You can play back up when I perform."

"I don't know. I really am not that good," I responded.

"I will show you what to do," He answered.

He reached into a case and handed me one of his flutes.

He told me; "Just follow my lead and play these notes up and down in the Background. I will play the lead music."

"OK!" I answered.

This was the first time I had ever played a flute in front of people. What a difference! The sounds were so deep and clear coming out through a speaker system. I realized that what I hear come out of the flute sounds different than what others hear. It is kind of like when you hear a recording of your voice and realize that it is different than what you think you sound like. The amplifier gives the flute an altogether different sound.

When we finished the presentation White Crow told the story of how the flute came to the people. It was a shortened version of the story. I thought about how the young boy was shown the flute by the woodpecker and the story related to respect for the woodpecker and gifting for the people. It was the first time I had heard anyone tell a native story in that way and I was impressed by the beauty in the way he told it. Everything that White Crow would say or do seemed to be surrounded by respect for everyone and everything around him. This man has that something that I am looking for, I thought.

About a month later I visited White Crow at his home. He made some adjustments to my flute that tuned it better and gave it a little more volume.

"The rest is up to you." He said. "Just be patient and let the flute teach you."

"How will I learn some songs?" I asked.

White Crow suggested; "Just play what you feel and the flute will teach you the songs to play. You can listen to flutists like Nakai and others and try to play their songs too if you want."

"Can you help me learn more about the people and the Spirit teachings?" I asked.

His answer was not what I expected but was honest.

He replied; "I don't know much. I am looking for someone to teach me too. There are not a lot of people here in New England who possess that kind of knowledge. I can help you with the flute but what you are seeking is more than I can offer when you ask about Spirit teachings."

It was good to have made this friend and I knew that our friendship would last for a long time.

Misho spoke, "I like it when you play the flute. So this man White Crow taught you, eh?"

Noodin replied; "He showed me some things but I think the most important thing is he gave me the legend of how the flute came to the people. That legend teaches one how to play in the story."

"Had you come into the circle at Zhinqwak's by then?" Misho asked.

"No! But it was about that time that I met Oshki."

Noodin went on; "My wife came to me one day and told me she wanted to get a dog."

"Nick has allergies, so what do you think about a Poodle?" She inquired.

"How big of a Poodle" I asked cautiously.

"A standard size", she replied.

I had grown up with Standard Poodles and they are great companions in a family. "They are a great dog", I answered.

That evening we went to meet Annie, a lady in town that breeds Poodles. She provided us with a pup that quickly became a part of our family. Sometimes I think the dog was my intended replacement. No matter! One of the benefits was that Annie also does grooming so an ongoing friendship would ensue between my wife and Annie. You, Misho, had adopted Annie's brother some years before. Annie told Monica about her brother Mike and his native experience."

Mike works for the US Air Force as a civilian contractor. He has something to do with surveillance equipment but very top secret. Not an Indian, Sicilian, he would proudly claim. He had learned from you and the Ojibwe for several years and had been given, gifted, a lot of knowledge. He is a sincere man with a good heart. At thirty something, Mike actually understood more of the Indian knowledge than most Indians. That was not real obvious at our first meeting though.

Noodin continued; "Monica told Annie that I followed Native American teachings and Annie arranged for Mike and me to meet. Mike's native name is New Life Way, Oshki Bimadiziwin [osh-key-bi-maadi-zi-win] in Ojibwe. We informally met at Annie's shop one day and kind of sized each other up a little. He seemed like a good man and sincere in his following. That was that!

I didn't see Oshki again for a long time. He was involved in his work and other pursuits and I was involved in mine. I was studying the Iroquois language and what teachings I could find from them. Oshki learned from the Ojibwe and I wanted my knowledge to come from one tribe so that I would not mix up different teachings. I chose the Seneca Nation of the Iroquois Confederacy. It seemed to me, though the teachings from one tribe to another are similar and point to the same reality of spirit on many levels, that learning from one tribe would be less confusing than mixing and matching. I felt that I would wait for that certain elder of the Seneca to suddenly appear."

Misho asked, "So when did you come to the first circle?"

Noodin replied, "It was a day in the fall when the phone rang."

It was Oshki; "Hi Jim, this is Mike Lamesa, you remember, Annie's brother. I know you follow native teachings so I wondered if you might be interested in coming to one of our gatherings."

"What kind of a gathering is it?" I asked. I was trying to seem knowledgeable even when I was not.

"We hold talking circles to honor Creator and learn from our Elders." Mike replied. "My Dad, Nagan way wedong, is visiting and we are holding a ceremony to honor him. Would you like to come?"

"Yes, that would be an honor. When and where?" I answered, trying not to sound excited.

Oshki explained where it would be and the time on Saturday night.

"You know," he added, "I have to drive my Dad down there. Maybe you could pick up my sister Annie and her son Mikie. They are coming to the ceremony and could direct you to Mike Jack Pine's place. Pick them up around six o'clock and you will have plenty of time to arrive there."

"That sounds fine to me." I answered. "I will see you there."

Noodin told Misho; "I was excited! I had actually been invited to attend a Native American ceremony! It wasn't Iroquois. It wasn't even a tribe from around here. I didn't know much about the Ojibwe Nation except that they historically had wars with the Iroquois.

Saturday came and I could not wait for six o'clock so I could pick up Annie and Mikie and go to the ceremony. When I arrived they were waiting and got into the car. We drove toward Groton, Massachusetts where Mike Jack Pine lived. Conversation was kind of light. I did not want to ask too many questions and show my ignorance. Annie didn't seem to know much about native things and was really going in support of her brother more than because this is something that she follows.

She knew you though, Misho. She told me you had been living out here with them and would have these circles every week. According to her, you had a large following of people that would come to learn from you. She said there was a woman that traveled with you named Doreena, but you broke up, and you were now traveling with a woman named Noreena. Annie was looking forward to meeting Noreena.

We arrived at Mike Jack Pine's house. There was a small group of people that had already arrived and they were standing around in the front yard, waiting to welcome you. A grey haired man came to the car, smiling and seemingly happy to see us there. Booshoo! He said. He gave Annie and Mikie a hug and then clasped my hand and gave me a hug.

I am Jim, "he said.

I was wondering at the time what he met by "booshoo". Why was he greeting me in what sounded like French.

"What is booshoo?" I asked.

"That is a greeting of hello in Ojibwe," he answered.

"It almost sounds French, like Bonjour," I answered.

He looked at me with a smirk. "No, he answered, it comes from the name of the first man, weno booshoo [way-no-boo-zhoo] and is used for a greeting by my people."

"Oh!" I answered; "boo – shoo."

"Ahow", he answered. "Booshoo!"

Jim introduced me around to the others. This is Althea. She is Ogallala Sioux. She looked down in a shy way as she said hello. She was dressed in a long dress with faded flower prints on it. She wore a shawl around her shoulders and didn't seem to want to talk.

Others in attendance were John and Rona. A couple from Massachusetts in their late fifties. They had been attending these ceremonies for a few years and were looking forward to seeing You again. Sussy and her husband Ken were there. Ken was part Iroquios and a flute maker and Sussy was a jewely artisan.

He then introduced me to Paul, who was a large man, somewhat older and not too stable on his feet. He smiled and shook my hand. Booshoo, he said in a quiet manner and I answered booshoo.

You were in your early sixties at that time, Misho, when I first met you.

We went in the house and Oshki introduced me to Mike Jack Pine, Zhingwak [Zhin-qwaak / White Pine] in Ojibwe. It was the name found for him by you, Misho, many years before. Zhingwak had a large house that was very appropriate for circles of eight to twenty people. He was a man in his sixties with thinning hair and was not Indian. When you went back to Minnesota a year before, Zhingwak continued the circle at his home.

I continued to attend the weekly circle for the next year while reading what I could about the Ojibwe people. The circle continued to go on as a small group, about five of us usually. We would practice language, read from different sources that offer teachings on traditional Native American culture and legends, and review teachings you had given to your group over prior years."

Misho said; "They did a good job. When I met you again, I thought you had been given teachings from someone else of the Ojibwe."

Noodin continued; "A year later, in the autumn of the year, we attended ceremonies at Pat's house in Ossipee. Pat Lillie has a home at a beautiful location on a lake near Ossipee, New Hampshire. There is a place by the lake to put a teaching lodge and sweat lodge leaving plenty of area for tents that people could stay in during the ceremonies.

Pat is keeper of a drum for the native people and has Micmac heritage. She is very particular about native tradition and opens her home to the native ceremonies to help the native people.

I still felt new to the circle but I was becoming committed to the teachings I was receiving. I still knew that an Elder would eventually come from the Iroquois so that I could learn from them. This experience would be helpful when that time came.

That year you came here. I went To Pat's on a Wednesday and was one of the first to arrive. You were somewhat aggravated that people were not arriving to help to prepare for the ceremonies. I still did not know you very well and felt somewhat intimidated by your presence. We had never talked at any length and you had only met me once at that first circle I had attended the year before. You were accompanied by Gary, a quiet native man who came to be your helper for the ceremony. There was much to do."

Misho said; "Everybody says they want to know, but nobody wants to do the work. The teachings are in the work."

Noodin continued; "First Gary and I prepared the fire pit. As others arrived, John, Rona, Oshki, Zhingwak and Sussy, we cut the poles for the lodge to hold ceremonies. We then constructed the lodge. It was built about 12' across and 20' long with a smoke hole cut through the center for smoke from the fire. The west end, or door, was closed off and people would enter through the door at the east end of the lodge. A wooden staff was put in the ground to the east of the fire to hold eagle feathers, referred to as veterans, during the ceremony. The lodge was covered with a large tarp. Part of the ceremony is the preparation, and you and others offered teachings to us while we constructed the lodge so we would understand the various reasons for doing these things in a certain way. It was a full day's work to prepare the lodge and it was a good opportunity for me to begin to know you better.

That night we would have a sweat lodge. The lodge was already built at Pat's and we covered it with heavy canvas tarp to block out any light from getting in. Mike arrived and asked me to help him to build the sweat lodge fire.

We gathered the grandfathers that would be used. Large grapefruit size rocks are used as the grandfathers. Then we set down seven logs on the ground of the fire pit so as to make two rectangle shaped areas joined together. Oshki explained the meaning of each stage of building the fire to me as we went along. Into the two areas we spread birch bark and then covered that layer with a floor of cedar shakes. On top of the cedar we put fire wood and set the first seven grandfathers. We then surrounded them with fire wood and more fire wood on top and then the rest of the grandfathers. Over the very top we put more fire wood. We then leaned fire wood all the way around and on top of the construction. It looked like it was going to be a big fire. When it was done, we waited until five o'clock. The lodge would begin at seven and it would take two hours to heat the grandfathers.

Oshki offered tobacco over the prepared fire with prayers for ceremony and thanks. He took a nest of dried grass and put it in a large shell. Then he held a piece of flint with a small piece of medicine, he called the medicine shkitaagan [shki-taa-gun / a birch fungus], in one hand and struck the flint with a piece of steel. The medicine lit on the first strike. Oshki fanned the medicine tucked into the nest of grass and the nest burst into flame. He then put the nest in a small hole beside the birch bark lined under the fire and the birch ignited. In a few moments a full blaze was going and flames were rising to about ten feet.

Oshki told me to stay with the fire and that if I needed to go anywhere, first, find someone to stay there since the fire should not be unattended. This was a teaching of how to prepare the fire for a lodge.

It was really impressive to see how this special fire was constructed. Now though, it is going to heat the rocks until they are red hot. Then, I thought, they expect me to go into the lodge with them. From what I had heard, it really heats up and it is hard to breathe. Some people can't take it and have to get out. I really didn't want to go in, much less have to ask to get out. I can't stand too much heat. Maybe I'll just pass when the time comes.

You came out and stood beside me Misho, watching the fire. You didn't say anything and neither did I. We just watched the fire for awhile. Oshki came up behind me and whispered, "You need to offer Misho tobacco to go into the lodge." "Oh", I answered. I reached in my pocket, took out a tobacco offering wrapped in red cloth and handed it to you. "I am giving you tobacco so that I can come into the lodge, I said." You accepted the tobacco and offered it to the fire.

Oh no! Now I am committed, I thought.

When the rocks were heated people started to show up wearing bathing suits or loose fitting dresses for the women. Oshki relieved me from watching the fire so that I could change into swimming trunks. When I returned another man was there. He would be our fire keeper. "This is Andy and he will watch the fire and bring in the grandfathers for us," Oshki said.

Misho, you stood in front of us and began to explain about the lodge and what would happen. First you indicated to each of us the order that we would enter the lodge. You would go in first, then Pat, John. Zhinguak, Athena, Rohna, Gary, Jim A., me and then Oshki. Andy will be our ishkode inninee [ish-ko-day i-ni-nee / fire keeper], you explained. You then continued: "The cedar that surrounds the lodge and is laid in a trail from the fire to the lodge must not be crossed by anyone except the fire keeper. When you go into the lodge, you should greet the lodge and tell the lodge who you are. Stay to the left of the cedar or life line when you go in and when you come out stay to the right of the life line."

It sounded like the rules of a chess game to me.

"We will line up and each of you will take tobacco in your left hand to offer to the fire with your prayers and then go into the lodge. Andy will smudge each of us with sage now and we will go in."

We lined up and Andy smudged each of us. As the smoke from the sage, used for the smudge, came before us, each one, in turn, motioned the smoke into our lungs and over our heads. We took our tobacco and offered our prayer with it to the fire. Then we crawled into the lodge. You called for the medicines and your drum. Then you asked for seven grandfathers to be brought in. It began to warm up as we greeted each of the grandfathers that came into the lodge. Then you called for the cedar water. A five gallon container of warm cedar water was brought in. You and Oshki took the container and held it over the fire four times and then set it down near you with a ladle for pouring the water onto the grandfathers. You then called for the door to be closed. It was totally dark now except for the soft glow of the grandfathers in the center hole called the center of the universe or womb of mother earth.

"Is everyone ready?" You asked. "Yes", we all answered. You added, "I run a gentle lodge. If anyone feels that they have to get out just say all of my relatives. The door will be opened then and you may leave. If you leave please wait quietly outside and concentrate on the ceremony going on in this lodge. I will now start."

Something was sprinkled onto the rocks and I could smell a pleasant fragrance fill the lodge. Each of us would watch the grandfathers as they would flash when the medicine was sprinkled over them. The flashes would seem to make different pictures appear and I would hear comments of; Oh look at that! And, did you see the wolf appear. Then all went quiet as the lodge began.

The lodge lasted about two hours and consisted of four sessions, or rounds. At the end of each round the door would be opened and more grandfathers would be brought in. The door would then be closed and the ceremony would continue. When the water had been poured and it was time to close the lodge, you made an offering to the directions and released the spirits that had come to help the people. You then told us that when the door opens everyone should go out in the same order they came in following you out the door. When out, each person would stand and face the western direction and give a yell to acknowledge the renewed life they have received through the ceremony."

"That was your first lodge Noodin?" Misho asked.

"Yes!" Noodin answered.

"What did you think of it?" He asked.

"To be honest, I thought I was going to die in there. It was so hot I could barely breathe. I had to put my head to the ground to find air and the heat felt like it was burning me inside and out. I couldn't understand why anyone would want to do this thing on a regular basis. When I left the lodge though, I felt fresh and full of new energy. It felt great but I did not look forward to doing it again. The next night, when asked if I was going in, I opted to be fire keeper. I remember telling you that I had a headache or something and did not feel up to going into the lodge.

I put the fire together the way Oshki showed me the night before and asked Oshki to light it. This striking of flint to make a fire seemed too difficult to me. He started the fire and I watched as the fire heated the stones to a bright red color. Everyone went into the lodge and I stood there waiting. Pretty soon you called out. "Pass in the medicines." I handed the medicines in. "Pass in the drums and shakers." I passed them into the lodge. "Bring in seven grandfathers," you said. I took the pitch fork used to pick the stones out of the fire and gathered a stone. "Grandfather coming in," I said. I could hear everyone in the lodge as the red hot stone came carefully into the lodge. "Booshoo Mishomis, Nokomis" [greetings grandfather, grandmother], they said. I gathered another stone and brought that one into the door of the lodge. "Booshoo Mishomis, Nokomis", they said with each stone that entered. The fire was hot and I could feel it burning my face and the hair on my arms was burning off. So this is why Indians don't have much body hair, I thought. Finally I had delivered seven grandfathers into the lodge. It was hard work! "Bring in the water!" Misho said. I handed in the five gallon container of cedar water and you lifted it to pass over the grandfathers with the help of Gary who was seated next to the door. Then you requested that the door be closed. I closed the door and everyone let me know when I had the door completely closed so no light could get into the lodge.

I stood outside the lodge watching the fire. It was a cool evening in October and the fire was nice to stand by but really hot when I had to go near to keep wood on top of the remaining stones. After a time

I heard you call out, "Ishkwan diem [ish-kwan-dame / door]!" I stood there for a few seconds and then heard you again. "DOOR! Open the door fire keeper!" I yelled back; "Oh!" I opened up the flap and steam came out so fast that I could feel the burning of the heat and had to lean away. You asked everyone if they were OK and they answered that they were fine. Everybody really seemed to be comfortable with all that heat. You asked for seven more grandfathers.

I went to the fire and gathered another stone with the pitchfork and passed it in. I gathered another and another and another. It was really hot going into the fire to gather those stones and I lost track of the number. "How many more?" I asked. "Three more grandfathers," Gary said. I passed in the remaining three and you instructed me to close the door once again. Again there was silence as the lodge continued.

I could hear talking in a low tone now and then as each person shared in the lodge. A drum started to play and someone began to sing a song in Ojibwe. Though I was standing next to the lodge, the song sounded as if it was being sung in a faraway place. It was a song of the ancient past coming through the night calling out all of creation to hear the people. I felt that I was standing alone in the universe by the fire and the star filled sky. The lake by the lodge was silent and peaceful with the reflection of the stars in the darkness of the still water. I felt drawn to be inside the lodge even though I knew the heat inside was intolerable. It was as if the lodge was alive and calling me to join in. I offered a prayer for the people inside and the spirits that were calling. I was deep in my thoughts."

You called out Misho; "Ishkwandiem! ISHKWANDIEM! DOOR! Doorman, open the door!"

I opened the door. Steam rolled out so fast I had to back away or be scalded from the heat.

You asked me; "Where were you? We have been calling."

I answered; "I was right here. I didn't hear you."

You said to me; "Pay attention! We are depending on you! We need more cedar water and three more grandfathers."

I complied with the request. Then I kneeled next to the door so that I would hear the next request. Some of the cedar water was passed around the lodge to give the people a drink. After all had taken a drink the cup was refilled and offered to me. "You are doing a good job and we are thankful you are there," you reassured me. I took a small drink of the cedar water and returned the cup. What was left was poured on the grandfathers and I was told to close the door for the next round. The third round passed without incident.

The fourth round was shorter than the rest and when the door opened each person came out. I would help each person to stand and welcome them back into the cool evening. Everyone was happy and seemed relaxed. There was laughing and singing as they covered themselves with blankets to stay warm in the night air.

Nothing more was ever said about my lapse in attention and Oshki told me that I had done good work. "We learn as we do the work," he said.

I realized that there was something more to the lodge than just going in and sweating through an unbearable heat. The lodge seemed to be doing something for the people. It seemed so easy for everyone else and yet I found it to be like torture. What was I doing or not doing that made it so hard?

The next night another fire was lit and another lodge was prepared. You came over and asked me if I was going in the lodge. I didn't want to, but felt that it was expected if I was truly dedicated so I reached into my pocket for tobacco to offer for a lodge. I really didn't want to do this thing and felt the pressure of the others, though no one would have given me pressure. I was doing it to myself. I knew I needed to do something different.

This time I listened closely once inside as you gave instruction before the door closed.

"Remember", you said, "You are here to make a sacrifice for others. You should be concentrating on your prayers to help others. Let the Spirits and Creator take care of you and stay focused on why you have come into the lodge."

As the lodge heated up I concentrated on my family, my friends and the people that had helped me to begin my walk. I thought of Tom Maize and White Crow and how they had guided me. With each round the lodge grew hotter than before and I concentrated as hard as I could on my wishes for a peaceful world and the wellness of others. When we sang I joined in and sang with all the voice I could gather in the heat. I tried to follow the strange words in the Ojibwe language of the song the best that I could.

I heard a voice call out, ishkwandiem, open the door. Everyone started to move toward the door to leave. "What was this," I thought.

"Don't we do four rounds", I asked, and Oshki replied; "we just did." I felt warm but I did not feel that it was a hot lodge like before.

As I came out the door I heard Zhingwak comment; "That was the hottest lodge I have ever been in."

I was beginning to understand, the lodge is not about me. It is about caring for the people. I felt like I had been touched while in that lodge. It was a calmness of presence I had only felt once before. Once when I was very young but I could not remember more than having had that feeling one time before.

We would close the ceremonies the next morning and all would depart for their homes and their busy lives. You, Noreena and Gary would start the drive back to Michigan.

When we left that lodge I knew that you, Misho, would be my teacher.

The next week I attended the circle with a new resolve to learn the teachings of the Ojibwe. I now realized that my prayer for an Elder had been answered. My teacher was to be you, an Ojibwe, not an Iroquois. It would be revealed in time that I had received an exact response to my prayer and that it was just as it should be.

The teachings that you gave at the ceremony and the notes you left with our circle made it easy to assimilate information. Digesting it and coming to understand the meaning has taken years and will continue to take years. The language was another thing altogether.

As I sat with you on that last day of the ceremony I remember what you told me."

Misho; "I remember that day. I told you that if I teach you, there is something that you must do. You must learn to speak Ojibwe. You see, when I tell you the stories of the people in English they only translate a little of what they carry. Kind of like reading Indian children's books, they tell in stores. They only give a little bit of the knowledge. I cannot share all of the meaning in English. If you understand the language, you will begin to see that each legend shares many teachings on different levels. You need to concentrate on the language of the people if you are to learn."

"Yes," Noodin answered. "We had looked at the language from time to time in the circle gatherings. We knew certain words. The names of some animals like bear / mukwaa, beaver / amik, bald eagle / mi gi zee and deer / wawa kay shee. We knew the names of the directions, the seasons, the medicines of spirit and the ages of man. This paled to the prospect of actually understanding and speaking the language."

Noodin commented; "I remembered my high school years. I was a terrible student at best and when it came to other languages, the barrier was too much. I took Spanish in the ninth grade and lasted a week. The school principal moved me out of Spanish and into French. That was worse, so they moved me into a general language course. The whole experience was like traveling to another planet where I would never be able to understand what was being said. I never considered learning any other language again and was grateful that I could even speak English. To learn to speak another language was beyond my capabilities and yet that is what I would have to do to be taught by you.

Before you left I told you that I would learn the language. I even dared the comment that I would be fluent in three years. I knew it would be impossible, but I really wanted to learn more from you so I made the commitment."

"You speak it pretty good now Noodin," Misho commented.

"Indo Ojibwemowin bungii et'igo. [in-do Ojib-way-mo-win bungee et-i-go / I speak Ojibwe language just a little]", Noodin responded. "And, it is more than three years since that time."

"Sometimes, you try too hard. You expect to get everything at once. Be patient Noodin, you have come a long way. The people like you." Misho said.

"Thank you Misho, I love the people." Noodin answered.

Chapter SIX

An Invitation

~**Amik**~ [beaver] Beaver demonstrates diligence in protecting the family and helping his brothers and sisters in the forest by demonstrating honesty in his work.

The trip back to Connecticut had been good for both Noodin and Misho. It was good after so many years to have time to spend really getting to know one another. All other times that Noodin had learned from Misho seemed to be amongst various groups of people and the two had never been able to focus on a one to one for any amount of time.

Both Noodin and Misho felt good to be getting to know one another on a more personal level.

The next morning Misho knocked on Noodin's door and invited him to breakfast. He had more questions and seemed genuinely interested in knowing how Noodin had come to know some of the things he knew.

At breakfast Misho asked; "Noodin when did you start attending the Midewiwin [Mi-day-wi-win / medicine society] Ceremonies run by Edie Benton?"

Noodin replied; "It was in 1999 or 2000 I think, Misho, but time seems to blend together as I learn and practice these things. I know it was at the time that you were going to initiate into that lodge. When we arrived at the Hannahville Rez in Michigan and Noreena's house, you were not there. There were some issues going on between you and her and you had gone back to Lake Lena to your home. With all that was happening you decided not to initiate that year and Oshki, John and I decided to help Noreena to go ahead with the trip to Bad River Rez in Wisconsin for the ceremony. Oshki drove Noreena's motor home, and John and I followed. We set up the motor home at the ceremony grounds and Oshki took my car and proceeded to find you.

John and I were not really aware of what was happening concerning you, Oshki and Noreena during that time.

My experience at the ceremony changed everything in my life and my understanding of centering in my life. We had traveled there to see you initiate but now the experience was more a matter of personal growth for John and me, since we had never attended anything like this. I will tell you my experience the way I feel that I experienced it.

This is what happened for me.

It was June of the year. The people of the circle in New Hampshire were invited by you, our teacher, in Michigan, to attend the spring Medicine Ceremonies in Wisconsin on an Ojibwe reservation. You were about 65 years old at this time and were to be inducted into the medicine society and you invited us to witness this ceremony. This recognition of our small circle in New Hampshire was a great honor to all of us. Three of the members of our band circle would make the journey. Oshki, John and I would make the 1,400-mile drive to Wisconsin.

We left New Hampshire early in the morning in late May to drive to Wisconsin. We took turns driving round-the-clock in order to arrive there in time. I found myself apprehensive as we traveled to Wisconsin. I had not been to a medicine ceremony. I had not been on a reservation or in a place where all of the people were a different culture and race than me. Questions were racing through my mind. Would these people accept a white man attending their cultural ceremonies? Would I do and say the right things? Was I just being foolish in trying to understand the spiritual relationship with my Creator in the ways of the American Indian? My mind was still filled with pictures of John Wayne chasing across the western prairies firing his Winchester rifle and Indians who were waiting with Tomahawks and shooting bows and arrows at the heroes who would win the west.

The medicine ceremonies were being held in an area of the reservation that had once been a Wisconsin State Park. When the park was closed the land was ceded back to the Indians and made part of the reservation. The camping areas were all heavily grown over with trees and brush and the people had cleared areas for tents and campers to be set up. We drove around the road until we came to a motor home belonging to your fiancée Noreena. There, we set up our three tents where we would live for the next five days.

After we had set up our camp, John and I walked up a hill to where the medicine ceremonies would be held. It was a large open area that is level near the top of a cliff overlooking Lake Superior. The medicine lodges would be placed in the center of this area. Sweat lodges were also placed nearby for use during ceremonies. We asked the fire keeper what we should be doing and he had John go to help get supplies. The fire keeper handed me a large ax and led me back down the road to where people were cutting firewood. He didn't say anything as we walked down the road and just seemed indifferent to me. The thought of chopping firewood after driving for twenty-five hours was somewhat disheartening but I joined the others and began to split firewood. Soon, one of the older of the young men that was working came over to me. He gave me a different axe and explained that I was using a cutting axe and it would be easier for me if I used a splitting axe. I didn't know they had different axes for splitting and cutting. We continued to chop wood for about an hour and everyone decided to take a break. I kept chopping wood because I was much slower at it than these experienced young men. One of them called over to me to take a break, and I said I didn't want to stop until I knew how much we would get paid for all this wood. Trying to be funny was not appropriate and one of the men commented that I must be using white man humor. Now I was embarrassed but at least I stopped to rest for a minute. We went back to it and after another hour or so completed the task.

We then began to load the wood onto a pickup truck to take up to the lodge area. A man about my age had been with us. His name is Peter and he was working with a chain saw cutting the wood into lengths as we were splitting. Now he was cleaning the chain saw to put away.

There was a young man in his mid thirties loading wood next to me. His name is Mark and he is about six feet tall and broad shouldered. As we were putting the wood on the truck Mark decided he would neaten the load by stacking the front area. I kept loading and after two or three pieces, managed to hit Mark in the arm. "Sorry about that," I said. He nodded okay and continued to work on the load. The next piece I loaded on hit him again. This time he stopped his work and squared off looking at me with a face full of fury and fists clenched. Everyone stopped working and watched as I looked back at this very pissed off Indian who was ready to do me in. I knew I had two choices. I could turn and run into the bush, never to be seen again or stand there and let this guy beat me to a pulp. It was obvious that I would be no match for him. Just at that point, Peter, who was cleaning the chainsaw, spoke up. "Mark," he said, "remember where you are." With those words the fists opened and the look of anger disappeared. Mark went back to work and I was much more careful putting wood on the truck. Finishing the work we parked the truck and quit for that day.

After the work was done I was a little tired but not nearly as much as I thought I would be. I went back to my camp to relax.

When I returned to the camp an Indian was standing there waiting for me. He had been watching as we cut wood earlier. He was a short heavyset man with a smile from ear to ear and very few teeth. He said to me: "I am Eddie but everyone calls me Pellie, aye, I am Loon Clan and we are camped next to you. Come join us at our fire. My brother's, Austin and Andrew, are there along with Andrew's girlfriend, aye".

I did not expect someone who I did not know to offer a hand in friendship so soon, if at all. I went over to the fire with no idea in my mind that I was about to experience something extraordinary. Austin, Eddie, and Andrew had traveled from Christian Island reservation in Canada. I would later learn that they are of the Beausoleil First Nation.[17] A place located about 150 kilometers (100 miles) north of Toronto.

Austin is a member of the medicine society and his brothers, Eddie, a.k.a. Pellie, and Andrew were there in support of the ceremonies.

---

[17] The Beausoleil First Nation is an Ojibwa (Chippewa) First Nation located in Simcoe County, Ontario, Canada. The Beausoleil First Nations occupies three Indian reserves. Their main Indian Reserve is the Christian Island 30 Indian Reserve, consisting of Christian Island, a large island in Georgian Bay close to the communities of Penetanguishene and Midland, Ontario, along with two other smaller islands. Together with the 7.5 hectares (18.5 acres) Christian Island 30A Indian Reserve located at Cedar Point, Ontario and the 3.1 hectares (7.7 acres) Chippewa Island Indian Reserve located in Twelve Mile Sound, 27.5 kilometres (17.1 mi) north of Christian Island, they form the land base for the Beausoleil First Nation. In September 2008, the Beausoleil First Nation had registered a population of 1798 people, of which 579 people lived on these Reserves

We sat by the fire and talked small talk for a while. Pellie looked to me and asked, "so why are you here, aye? What do you want to know? We will answer all your questions for you."

I sat for a minute and thought of all the questions I had to ask; What are your beliefs? What makes this so special? What magic do you know about spirituality? Do all Indians still follow this way? Do you see the spirits in your life and many more questions? It was as if the questions I would have were coming to mind in a rush. There was so much I wanted to know.

As I began to speak of things that I wanted to know, Austin looked across the fire and stopped me. "Jim," he said, "stop for a minute. You have so many questions. Stop thinking so fast in your mind, your heart can't keep up." Austin's comment stopped me in my tracks. I hardly knew what to say next. I knew what he was saying to me. He was telling me if I would simply listen humbly and watch respectfully then all of my questions would be answered. I stopped with my questions and smiled across the fire at Austin. "I understand," I said.

What happened next would change my life. Austin looked at me and stood up to walk around fire. He came up behind me and leaned down and spoke into my ear. "Jim, you have done much in your walk of life to find your center. There are two things that you need to do that you have not yet done. You need to apologize to your mother and father for the things you did and you need to apologize to the Creator." With that he walked back to his place by the fire and sat down.

I looked at him smugly and said, "I don't understand, I've processed my feelings for my parents and Creator. Why do I need to apologize?" Austin answered: "This is what I know." I thought about what he said for a few minutes and it began to dawn on me that I had forgiven my parents for the things that happened to me in my life because I realized they always did the best they could. It was really not their fault they were not perfect and they had always done the best they could for me. I had also forgiven Creator, for all the things in my life I could not understand and was unhappy with because I thought it was Creators fault those things were put there in my path. Yes, in my mind I had done all I needed to do. So why did Austin think I should apologize?

Then it hit me. He was right! I looked across the fire at Austin and told him, "you are right". Austin responded: "Then you need to stand at the fire and offer your prayers and tobacco." I stood up, feeling a little silly, and took tobacco from a can of tobacco I had and looked at the fire. I said to myself, "Mom and Dad I am sorry. Creator

I am sorry for the way I have spoken about different beliefs and you." I put my tobacco in the fire and sat back down.

Then Austin said to me: "Tomorrow you need to go down to the beach and walk up to the point a few miles from here. As you walk, watch the water and you will see two grandfathers in the water. Gather those grandfathers and take them with you when you go back to the east. They are waiting for you and they are to be your teachers." I listened to Austin and I accepted what he said but I thought this was going a little far. I thought, "How did he know that I had not apologized to Creator or to my parents when I had done an inventory of my life to find balance? How did he know that?" Maybe it is just one of those things, you know, when people tell you things that are fairly obvious and you sit there and say; Wow, how did they know that? When anybody could have figured it out and it might have applied to a lot of people as easily as it applies to you. Then again he was pretty direct about what I needed to be doing and why. As a matter of fact, he was also right on.

The next morning was a time to build the lodge. Chopping wood was my first task and John was out cutting poles to build a lodge. Most of the people had not arrived. The ceremony would run Wednesday through Sunday. The fire would be lit Thursday morning and the ceremony would begin then. The ceremony really begins with the preparation of the ceremony grounds. For some the ceremony began when they came to mow the area and pick up debris around the area. As people arrived and began to work, the ceremony began for them. When John and I began our work the ceremony was in motion for us. The next morning, Wednesday, called camp day, is the day that everything is supposed to be prepared for the ceremony.

John and I went over to the place where the lodge would be built and began to help to set and bend poles that would be tied into the form of a lodge. A large structure built about 35' wide and 120' long. The main lodge would be covered and would be for ceremony and the fire. A second lodge was being constructed, like the first only it would not be covered. That lodge is for the induction of new members of the lodge. We did anything we could to help in the construction and preparation. As more and more people came and pitched in, there became less and less for us to do.

Now and then they would ask us to help with something if no one else was handy, but it was obvious that we were being crowded out. Some of the people were friendly enough and others would act as if we were not there. It was obvious that there are a lot of mixed feelings over the presence of Oshki, John and me. Most of the people there are from various Indian reservations in the United States and Canada. Some of the people were having difficulty accepting that white men were helping with the lodge. After all, this ceremony is native and not for everybody.

Misho said; "These ceremonies are the ones that were given to us by Creator for us to use. In this time of things coming together it is good that you are there. Many of the people would not agree with that though.

I invited you so that you could see the value of what you are learning and how it helps the people.

What else did you experience there Noodin?"

THE TOBACCO! If the experience of meeting Austin and his brothers had been the only experience of the ceremony, it would have been enough. The first day of the ceremony begins at sun rise with the lighting of the ceremony fire. Everyone attends and there were about three hundred native people present. The fire keepers prepare the fire by setting up the sticks in a teepee form in the fire pit. The men each pick up two thin sticks from a pile set at the side of the fire and gather in a circle around the fire. The chief fire keeper then begins to hit the sticks together in a beat like a drum and to sing a song asking for the spirits to come and begin the ceremony. All of the men join in hitting their sticks together with the beat set by the chief and to sing the song for the fire. A fire keeper then strikes flint and starts an ember in a nest of grass. He fans the ember until the nest ignites. It is then put into the fire. As this is being done the people with the sticks chant and hit the sticks together to make a clicking drumming sound. It does not take more than a minute to get the fire that is desired. The people with the sticks then add them to the fire and the fire keeper adds more wood to build the ceremony fire.

As I stood there watching this event it was amazing to me that so much respect and acknowledgement would be given to the lighting of a fire. But then, this was not an ordinary fire as I would come to understand in time.

The ceremony continued and a bowl was passed to collect tobacco from the people. I stood there feeling somewhat uneasy knowing I had not brought any tobacco. As the bowl was brought around a man tapped me on the shoulder and offered me some of his tobacco to put into the bowl. I was grateful to this man for saving me from embarrassment. When I turned to thank him I realized it was the same man that had saved my bacon when chopping fire wood. It was Peter from the wood cutting the day before

The ceremony continued and when it was completed the people began to leave the lodge going from the south side of the lodge to the west end, making a tobacco offering to the fire, and walking out the eastern entry of the lodge. Again I had no tobacco and again Peter handed me some tobacco. "You really need to carry tobacco in a pouch", he commented as we walked out.

I knew what had to be done. I needed to find some buckskin and thread and make a tobacco pouch, but where? I went back to our camp and asked Noreena if she had any buckskin. "What do you want it for?" She asked. I told her what had happened. "I need to make a pouch for my tobacco", I said. "I don't have any buckskin", she said, "but wait here." She went into the back of her motor home and came back with a beautiful buckskin pouch. It had not been used and had a Crane painted on it and long tassels of leather. It was the most beautiful pouch I had ever seen. "Take this", she said. "No, I can't", I answered. "Take it", she said, "I have others and this one needs to go with you." I accepted it and gave her a hug. How could she be so generous?

I found my can of tobacco and filled the pouch. When ceremony started again I went back to the lodge, hoping to find Peter who had now helped me three times. As I looked for him he came up behind me and tapped me on the shoulder. I turned and he introduced himself. "My name is Peter", he said, "This is for you." He handed me a leather pouch filled with tobacco. "Miigwich [me-gwitch / thank you", I said. "Where did you get it?"

He answered; "I made it in my camp after the last ceremony. Figured you should have a pouch of your own if you are going to attend ceremonies".

I thought to myself, "is this tobacco so important, really?" I understood that it is to offer prayer to Creator and I even knew the Legend of Asema [ah-say-maa / tobacco], the man who would live forever in the form of tobacco to carry the prayers of the people. There are so many legends about the tobacco. Stories how bald eagle saved the world when he saw a grandfather and grandmother showing their grandchildren how to offer tobacco, the story of the Four Chiefs and many others.

To me tobacco was important in order to offer prayer because it was what my new found friends did. I knew that any prayer to Creator is heard by Creator and that tobacco was just a kind of visible sign. Indeed, we can always talk to creator and the many Spirit helpers of Creator. So what is the big deal about tobacco?

Now I find myself frantically running around trying to find a pouch and making sure my tobacco is always available. I am offering tobacco in fires at the camp, at the ceremony, in the water at the lake and to the ground when I get up. What I am watching others do is having a personal effect on me. I suddenly find that a little tobacco adds to the importance of the prayer I offer. Knowing the teachings of tobacco make me realize that the prayers I offer are being answered immediately by Creator. It's kind of like email compared to, so called, snail mail through the post office. I think the prayers offered to Creator are recognized by Creator directly from our heart and yet making this simple offering allows the added confidence that the prayer was given with the best possible acknowledgement of creator and in all sincerity.

This man Peter gave me the first of the teachings of tobacco. Others had informed me of tobacco and I understood the traditional offering of tobacco when asking something of someone, or giving thanks to someone for a deed that they have done. The traditional use of tobacco seemed more like a trade to me before Peter offered me his tobacco. I gave tobacco to learn about the flute and in trade my friend White Crow shows me how to play and tells me how the flute came to the people. Kind of like money is the way I used tobacco. I give an Elder tobacco and he lets me into a sweat lodge.

Peter helped me realize the importance of acknowledgement in prayer and it started with tobacco, a pipe and a fire. Through history, all spiritual beliefs use offerings to go with prayer. It never made sense to me until now. Maybe it confused me because of some of the things people of other faiths used for offerings like virgins, lives of enemies, animals and such.

The next day I was at the ceremonies watching all the things going on. The sun was high and it was getting hot, so I decided to take a break and go for a walk. I figured that this was as good a time as any to walk down the beach. I climbed down the embankment about 150 feet from the top to bottom, took off my shoes and began to walk down the beach. It was a beautiful day and the water was calm and clear as glass. There were groups of stones here and there in the water. I was not sure what a grandfather would look like or if I would recognize one if I saw one. The stones on that beach were all different colors, sizes and shapes. They were so pretty that I couldn't resist picking some up for my kids at home.

Both Nick and Steph love to collect stones. I remember thinking, if I find one of those stones, a grandfather, I'll take it home and give it to my son. He would like to have that. If I find two I can give the other one to my daughter and she will like that.

While in my thoughts and collecting the rocks I had walked nearly a mile down the beach. I glanced out into the water and saw a beautiful round gathering of colored stones. The gathering was perfectly round and looked like a beautiful table top with all imaginable colors. I stopped and walked a few feet into the water and looked closer because it was such a pretty sight. Then I could see, right in the middle of the gathering of stones, a perfectly round stone about two inches in size. I walked out a little further and reached down into the middle of the gathering and took that stone, that grandfather. I held it in my hand and I looked at it and I couldn't believe how perfectly round it was. I noticed that all around that rock there was a line as if someone had carved it outlining into it exactly a straight cut all the way around the stone. I thought to myself, "This is really an amazing stone." I then continued to walk down the beach and I looked even harder than I had before but there was nothing there.

Eventually I reached the point a few miles down the beach from where I started and I turned to walk back. I was walking back and was about halfway. I could just barely hear the sound of the water drum at the ceremony and knew that another person was being inducted to the medicine society. I looked into the water and again I saw another beautifully colored gathering of stones. This was the same as before but further out in the water. Again in the middle of those colored stones was a perfectly round stone looking as if it had been placed there on purpose. It was a beautiful round stone, a little bigger than the one I had found before and the line wasn't quite as deep that traveled around that grandfather. I had to go waist deep in the freezing water of Lake Superior this time. I reached down and tried to keep my head out of the cold water but could not reach the stone. Finally I put my head under water and reached for the stone.

After I retrieved that grandfather from the water I walked up onto the beach. I took the two grandfathers that I had collected, one in each hand, and I stood on the beach. Suddenly I felt my skin grow cold and tingly. I began to sweat and I felt light headed. The faint sound of the water drum, so far away, became loud as if the drum were right there where I was standing. It was like some sort of energy was surging through me from those two stones. I felt a sudden urgency that I needed to say I was sorry to my parents and Creator. My emotions overcame me and I was completely in tears and shaking and I knew what Austin wanted me to know. I looked into the sky and cried out loud to my mother and father "I AM SORRY FOR THE THINGS THAT I DID THAT HURT YOU", and I could sense in my heart that they heard me. I said to Creator; "I AM SORRY FOR THE WAYS I OFFENDED YOU AND I WILL NOT DO THESE THINGS ANYMORE," and I knew that Creator heard me.

After that, still in tears, I walked down the beach and back to the path that led to the ceremonies. As I stood there watching the ceremonies and looking at the people, I came to realize that I was watching things that have been happening for these people for thousands of years. The people I met at the ceremonies are first in relationship with their spirits and then to all of the things in the world. With all that they have faced over the years as a people they are still filled with love for all things, respect for all things and an understanding of who they are, where they've come from and where they are going."

"What happened to those stones", Misho asked?

"I have them in my bundle. One of them helps me understand my ancestors. The other brings me dreams when I sleep with it."

"They are medicine stones. Be careful how you use them Noodin." Misho said.

CHAPTER SEVEN

Finding a Name

~ *Zoon gide'iwin* ~ **[bravery]** Bravery to do things even in the most difficult times. Be ready to defend what you believe and what is right. Always stand up for the people.

In early spring the changes on Mt. Monadnock, in New Hampshire, are often dramatic. The hiking trails begin to melt off the ice that has built up during the winter and the trails near the base soften as the saturated mud warms. Each step one takes becomes a test to see if the ground is firm. A step on the soft path will often result in a gusher of muddy water squirting up from hidden pockets in the ground. Melting water comes down the trails making them streams to be traversed by the hikers anxious to climb the mountain. The trees barely have buds and yet those hints of budding new life will quickly form and fill the forest with lush shades of green between the groves of evergreen that dominate the forest scene.

At the summit one can see out over five states from this mountain that stands alone. The panoramic view is awe inspiring and more than one hundred thousand hikers traverse this beautiful mountain each year to experience the beauty and energy of this place. It has been said that the word Monadnock derives from an old Indian word meaning mountain that stands alone. Geologists today use the term Monadnock to describe any mountain that stands by itself.

This is the home for Noodin. In the winter he lives in a lodge in the state park at the base and in the summer he camps amongst the campers that come to enjoy the serenity of the beautiful forest.

Noodin had not seen Misho during the winter. Misho returned to Lake Lena Reservation after his trip to Massachusetts where they had last visited with one another.

This early in the spring Noodin still lived in the cabin along the White Dot Trail. The weather can change at any moment from calm spring breezes to freezing storms of snow, ice or rain. The winds on the mountain are often strong at this time of year. Some winds come through that may have gusts up to eighty miles an hour or more.

Misho's red truck came up the long entry road to the park toll gate where he was greeted by a ranger. He told the ranger that he was looking for Noodin. The ranger took his two way radio off his belt and keyed up. "72-22 to Noodin" he said into the radio. "10-3" came a reply over the radio. "You have a visitor. Shall I send him up", the ranger inquired? "10-5, yes. I will wait for him in the top lot.", Noodin answered. "10-5" the ranger responded. The Ranger then directed Misho to continue up the road to the parking area.

Noodin built a fire in the fire place in anticipation of Misho's arrival and had coffee freshly made. Misho would only stay for a day or so. Noodin wanted to have all the time he could to visit during Misho's stop over.

They greeted one another and went to the cabin. Misho sat on a wood stool near the fire and seemed so relaxed that one might think he had been resting there for the whole day rather than driving all night to get there.

"You have a comfortable lodge Noodin. Do many people come to visit you here?"

"Thank you Misho. Yes! A lot of people do. This cabin serves me well but I still have too many things. The more I give away the more people bring to me. I have to protest some of the gifting because people think I need more things.

The people that visit me often are seeking to know how I survive up here on the mountain. They think I live in hardship or something. I don't know. They want to know what I have learned from you and others of the native people.

It is interesting, Misho to see how much people want to know."
Noodin said. "I am no different than anyone else, I guess. It is just
human to expect everything to come at once. You know, I really have
been patient about some things as I have walked this road. When I talk
to people some of the things that they ask are: how can I build a sweat
lodge, can you give me an Indian name, where can I get a eagle feather
and can I buy a pipe like the one you have. People have no idea of
what it takes to accumulate these sacred items and the requirement of
personal sacrifice for the people that is involved."

Misho; "They always ask but they don't wait to hear the answers
and if they do wait they don't listen."

Noodin; "We are in a time of instant gratification and if it
doesn't work just throw it away. This road I am walking tells me
something different. Accept the things that come in the time that
they come. Be happy with what I have in the present. Material
things are nice but they are also a burden that must be cared for and
protected. It is better to gift the things that you have than to have
too much. All that we really need, we have through Creator and the
basics of food, shelter and clothing are the only material things we
really need."

Misho asked; "How are you coming with the language?"

Learning the language has always been difficult for Noodin.
Going to that first ceremony at Pat Lillies' increased Noodin's resolve
to be able to speak Ojibwe.

As Noodin began to speak he looked over at Misho and could see
that he had fallen asleep. He had probably been driving much of the
night to get to Noodin's home.

Noodin thought about Misho's question and remembered the year
that he built a teaching lodge for Misho at Pat lillie's place in Ossipee,
New Hampshire.

It was a year after that first ceremony before anything of
significance and personal growth happened again. Noodin went to
some powwows, usually alone. He went to maybe two or three Sweats
at Pat's lodge and did some fire keeping for her. He always went to
circle each week and saw John, Zhinguak, Rona, and Sussy.
Sometimes Oshki was there too. Noodin worked on learning the
language of Ojibwe and found it totally confusing with nothing other
than tape recordings and a dictionary to learn from.

Difficulty in learning the language was compounded by a number
of factors. Noodin has a thirty percent hearing loss stemming from his

time in military service during Vietnam. He cannot hear all sounds. Sounds are critical in the language of the Ojibwe.

The language also has many different dialects, hundreds to say the least. Some of what Noodin would gather would come from one dialect and other teachings of the language would be given in different and varied dialects.

Austin, Noodin's adopted brother, once told him; "Speak slowly because you speak in different dialects mixed together and we have to think about what you are saying in order to understand."

In the fall it was time once again for the summer ceremony to take place at Pat's and that was when Noodin truly began to feel that Misho was indeed his Elder teacher. Pat gave out the dates to be at ceremony and Noodin couldn't wait for the time to come. He made sure he was there on the first day early so Misho would have enough people to do the work. Misho had been there at Lake Ossipee, New Hampshire for a couple of days with Gary. When Noodin arrived it was just Misho, Pat, and Gary doing the work.

Misho was sad that others had not made an effort to be there but went ahead with the commitment to ceremony. The four of them sat down to decide how to proceed and Misho looked at Noodin and said "build the lodge".

"What?" Noodin answered.

"Build the lodge", Misho repeated.

"I don't know, Misho. I've never built a lodge." Noodin replied.

"You helped last year and you have seen how they are built haven't you? You also helped build the lodge at Bad River eh?" Misho persisted.

"Well, yes, but it is a little different when I have to build it myself. " Noodin continued to protest.

"You will have Gary to help and others will be coming. This needs to be done today before darkness", said Misho indicating some urgency.

"OK, but what if I don't build it right?", Noodin answered.

"Then I will tear it down and you can build it over again." Misho answered.

Then Misho, Gary and Pat laughed.

Gary and Noodin went up a hill across the road from Pat's house to cut saplings for the lodge frame. Noodin found a grandfather Maple Tree and asked for the saplings with prayers and tobacco. They took the saplings they needed and returned to the area were the council lodge would be constructed.

By the time they returned, John was there to help. It took about an hour and a half to build the frame for a council lodge and cover it with canvas. They prepared the council fire pit and brought in chairs for the people. The lodge was not that large – about 15 feet by 24 feet. Large enough for twenty or thirty people. Misho inspected the work and decided it did not need to be torn down and rebuilt.

That evening Misho had a circle and sweat lodge. The next morning was a sunrise ceremony and the lighting of the sacred fire in the council lodge. Everyone had breakfast after the ceremony and agreed to start the teachings around eleven in the morning. It would be a good day.

In the traditional way, one learns by watching others, doing work and listening to the oral teachings. It was around ten thirty when Oshki and Misho brought in their sacred items to lay out their bundles. As pipe carriers it is expected that your items will be out for use during the ceremony.

Noodin knew this but did not realize that only the pipe carriers would put out bundles. Most people he knew have a bundle. Zhinqwak always would bring out his bundle and put it down and he is not a pipe carrier. Noodin assumed that it was the correct thing to do to put out his bundle. So he went to his car and gathered his bundle and brought it in and laid it out in front of his place in the lodge.

Noodin put all of the items that he considered to be sacred from his bundle out on his cloth very carefully as he had seen the others do. He felt the pride of knowing what to do and of all that he had learned over a few years from his brothers amongst the Ojibwe. It was at that point that Misho walked into the lodge.

"What is that in front of you Jim", Misho asked?

Noodin looked up at Misho and answered, "That is my bundle Misho."

"Why do you have it out in here?" Misho asked.

"Well, I thought if we had our bundle with us we were supposed to put it out for ceremony", Noodin answered.

"Only if you are going to use it in the ceremony, Jim. These things that are laid out by Oshki and me are going to be part of the ceremony." Misho explained.

There were about ten people sitting in the lodge at this point and Noodin was feeling really embarrassed but tried not to show it.

"I will put it away then, Misho. I didn't know!" Noodin responded.

Misho told Noodin; "Leave your bundle out."

Misho stood up and walked around the lodge to the place where Noodin was sitting and kneeled in front of him. He looked at the blanket and the items Noodin had laid on it.

Misho picked up a bullet that Noodin had laid on the blanket and asked; "What is this?"

"It is a bullet; it reminds me that I am a veteran and that I carry a white bundle as well as this one." Noodin answered.

"Put that away! It is a weapon and does not belong in the bundle", Misho said.

Misho picked up a pipe stone turtle and looked at it. "What is this?"

"It was given to me by my daughter and reminds me of the four directions and that we are here on Turtle Island", Noodin answered.

Misho put it back and picked up a miigas [me-gaas / Conch] shell. "What is this?" Misho asked?

"It is a miigas shell. It reminds me of the medicine society and the seven fires. The great migration that followed the shell to the west." Noodin answered.

"Take it out of your bundle Jim. That does not belong to you", Misho said.

By now Noodin is beyond embarrassed and just taking whatever comes as Misho continued to go through his bundle taking every other thing in it out, and explaining why it should not be there.

Noodin realized that he was being given a tremendous teaching, along with onlookers, about just what a sacred bundle is and why it is the way that it is.

As Noodin looked up at Misho he saw that Misho had tears streaming from his eyes. "I don't want to hurt you, Jim. I am trying to help you know the things I have to share. I am sorry that I am hurting you."

"I know Misho. I understand. Thank you for helping me." Noodin answered.

Noodin felt bad for his teacher, that he had put him in this place.

The ceremony began and after opening the ceremony with prayers the teachings began. Misho stood and started to speak. In his hand he held two beautiful Golden Eagle feathers.

Misho spoke, "When I was in the army they used us as radio men and had us speak our language on the radio in Korea. Two other brothers from my reservation and I would work together and travel with our company to provide radio contact.

One day our squad started to cross a field at dusk. As we reached the middle of the open field, a machine gun started firing from the other side. When it stopped, I was the only one standing in that field. Everyone in the squad had been killed, including the two brothers I had grown up with.

From that time to this I have carried these two Golden Eagle feathers in my bonnet to remember my fallen brothers. "

As Misho spoke he began to walk slowly around the circle.

"There is a time when everything must travel and it is time for these veterans to travel." Misho said.

As Misho said this he walked by Noodin and put one of the two feathers in his hand. Misho continued until he reached Gary and put the other feather in his hand. Misho then went back to his place and a pipe was smoked.

Misho finished saying, "it is sometimes a hard thing to let something go. It is important to know when to hold on and when to let go." That was the teaching.

Noodin sat there with tears in his eyes that Misho would honor him in such a way. He never would have expected to be gifted such a precious and meaningful gift from his red brothers.

As Noodin sat there his mind thought of all the beautiful things that had happened to him since he began to walk this path. He thought of all of the teachings that were gifted to him in his life and how much he desired to be able to gift back to his brothers and sisters on this road, the red road. How could he ever repay even the smallest of kindnesses that he had received?

When the gathering broke for lunch Noodin thought about that feather. "I don't even know who I am to Spirit world, he thought."

Noodin never asked about his name because he felt that he would know the time when that information would be forthcoming and he would simply wait.

Some knew Noodin as Niswiimiikanung [ni-swee-mee-ka-nong / three paths] but that was a name he was called because of how he had come to the circle. It was basically his Indian name.

Everyone has a name known in Spirit world and that the Spirit world recognizes an individual by. Many go through their lives not knowing that name or that it may even exist. That is the name Noodin did not know.

Now Noodin was carrying a veteran, a Golden Eagle Feather, and didn't know his Spirit name. Noodin thought about this and realized that this was the time he should seek this name. The responsibility of that feather represents caring for the people as a protector. Among the people there is no greater honor that can be bestowed on a person.

Noodin found where Misho was sitting and sat by his side.

"Misho", Noodin said. "I am offering you tobacco with a request. You have gifted me a great honor. To accept such a gift I feel that I should know who I am known as by Spirit world. Can you find out what my name is?" As Noodin said this he handed Misho a pinch of tobacco to go with the request.

Misho casually answered; "I will see what I can do and let you know."

That evening the people at the gathering went into a sweat lodge. As the lodge went into its second round Noodin could feel the heat building and the sweat was coming off him like a river. He focused as hard as he could on his prayers and the words that were being offered. Noodin listened to Misho as he spoke in his language and could almost understand a lot of what he was saying. He heard Misho send out his spirit helpers to ask for something and then Noodin saw a bluish light circle around and go out of the lodge through the top. The round finished and the door opened to invite more grandfathers in for the third round.

As the third round began and the door closed. The heat came back into the lodge almost at once. As the people offered their prayers, Noodin felt as if a wind was blowing the hot air around and he opened his eyes. That is when he saw it. A blue light entered like a group of stars into the lodge from the back, the west door of the lodge. It came in and went to the top of the lodge and seemed to circle and then it came toward Noodin and over his head, and disappeared somewhere behind him.

When the lodge was finished Noodin walked a little way away from the fire and sat on a bench to dry off and put on some clothes. He was thinking about what he had just seen and felt.

Misho came over and sat down beside him. They each lit a cigarette.

"I know who you are, Jim." Misho said.

"You do?" Noodin answered.

"What did you feel in that lodge?" Misho asked.

"I felt like there was a wind blowing and I saw a blue light that came in and went behind me." Noodin answered.

"The blue light came in and went right over your head and stayed there." Misho said.

"Your spirit name is Noodin, Wind." Misho announced.

"We will have a naming ceremony tomorrow. You need to find a man and woman to sponsor you. They will help you when you need them." Misho instructed Noodin.

"Thank you Misho, for giving me a name." Noodin said.

Misho looked down at the ground with a disappointed look. "Jim, you haven't learned anything. You don't know nothing! I didn't give you a name! That is your Spirit name! It is the name that you are known by in Spirit world and has been your name since the beginning of creation. You carried that name into this realm and will carry it with you when you go over to the next realm and for as long as the creation exists. You need to pay attention to these things!" Misho scolded.

That evening, as Noodin lay in his camper trying to go to sleep, he thought about who he would ask to be his sponsors.

Noodin decided Pat would be a good woman sponsor since he knew her to be a tough, tell it like it is kind of woman. Learning to respect women came hard to Noodin and she would keep him on the straight and narrow.

For the man Noodin's mind went to Peter who he came to know at the medicine ceremonies. He thought of all Peter had done to look out for him even before they really knew each other. The teachings he had given Noodin about prayer and tobacco. There was no question in Noodin's mind that Peter was the man that would support him.

The next morning Noodin asked Pat and she agreed. Noodin called Peter at his home on Six Nation Reserve in Canada.

Phone call to Peter. "This is Jim." Noodin began.

"Booshoo, Jim, how are you?" Peter answered.

"I am fine Peter. I am at ceremony in New Hampshire and I am offering you tobacco for something." Noodin explained.

"What is it that you need, Jim?" Peter answered.

"Misho, my teacher, has found my Spirit name and I need a man supporter. Would you stand up for me?" Noodin asked.

"That is a really important thing that you are asking of me, Jim. I don't know if I can because I am a Midewiwin. Let me think about it and I'll get back to you." Peter exclaimed.

Noodin knew that it might take a long time for Peter to get back to him. He is a dedicated and humble individual. Though Peter would want to do this, he would also want to be sure that he was doing the right thing.

Noodin also knew in his heart that Peter was the one. There was no one else that could do this for him. Noodin trusted what he knew and told Misho that he had asked, and that Peter would let him know. He told Misho he already believed Peter would be the one and was sure about this.

The ceremony continued and Misho went ahead with the naming that day.

About six weeks went by and Noodin received a call from Peter.

Noodin answered the phone: "Booshoo Peter, aanii easha ayaayung?" [Boo-zhoo Peter aa-nee aye-zhaa-aa-yaa-yong? / Greetings Peter, how are you]

"Nimii nu ayaa, miigwich". [ni-mee new aa-yaa, me-gwitch / I am fine, thank you.] Peter responded.

"About sponsoring your name." Peter went on. "I asked some of my friends what they thought about me being your name sponsor. A lot of them felt that I shouldn't do it because you are not Indian. Others said it didn't matter much but they wouldn't do it. There were other people that didn't see anything wrong with it.

Finally I called Eddie Benton, the Midewiwin Grand Chief, and asked him what he thought. Eddie asked me if you are a good man and sincere in learning these ways. I told him that you are. Then Eddie said that there was a time when the white man lived very much like us and had teachings that were very similar. These teachings, he said, were lost to the white man a long time ago. If this man has come to seek information to regain the knowledge of this spirit bundle then we cannot deny that to him.

"It is sad", Eddie added, "that more have not come asking to know these things."

I will be your name sponsor, Noodin."

Miigwich nikaang Ozhibige Inini. [Mee-gwitch ni-kaang O-zhi-bi-gay in-ni-nee / Thank you my brother Story Writing Man.]

CHAPTER EIGHT

A Family – A Clan

~**Mukwa**~ [bear] Bear permitted Weno Booshoo, first man, to continue his journey because of his bravery in facing him.

The morning had gone by quickly and Noodin prepared some wild rice and leftover meat from the dinner the night before. It was plenty for Misho and Noodin.

Misho asked; "Noodin. Tell me about your clan. You call yourself Loon Clan but I do not remember you asking me to find your clan. How did you come to be Loon Clan?

"I am Loon Clan, Misho. By adoption. In Celtic tradition I am Bard Clan. I claim both clans." Noodin answered.

"How did you come to know your clans, Noodin? Did you just pick a clan or what?" Misho asked.

Noodin answered; "The Celtic clan was not too difficult to figure out. My last name, Beard, is a derivative of the name Bard. So somewhere back in the past my name came from the Bard name.

The Bards were a clan of the Celtic People[18] and are documented to some extent. They were known as a chieftain clan, a story telling clan and as ambassadors of sorts in various parts of Europe. Evidence of the Bards is found in England, France and Germany as far as I know.

I have always had an interest in knowing my heritage and fortunately there have been historians in my family that have maintained records of my family tree. We have records of generations that date back to the late thirteenth century."

Misho spoke; "'So the Bard Clan is a Celtic Clan? It is your white bundle then, right?"

Noodin answered; "Yes! In a manner of speaking. The information available about those teachings are very sketchy in my view. Though I seek information on those teachings I find that the teachings from you and my red brothers are much more complete, intact and meaningful.

Noodin went on; "The Loon Clan came in several ways. As if Spirit were guiding me to it.

When I first came to New Hampshire in the late eighties and Monica and I had children, I began camping in earnest with my family. The first place that we went to camp was a state park, Pillsbury State Park. It is a beautiful place and I mentioned it to you before. The camping there is primitive. We were given a site down a path and near the water. It was our first camping trip with the kids. A hurricane was predicted for that night, but in the early evening it was quiet and peaceful. We went to sleep in our tent and sleep came quickly. Suddenly there was a loud shrill noise that broke the silence and woke both Monica and me from our sleep. It came again and was eerie to hear. The sound was followed by a series of shrill cries that sounded like voices heckling in a menacing or somehow wicked manner. Like witch's screaming and menacingly laughing in the night. We did not know what the noise was and had not camped in New England before, so every sound in the forest was unfamiliar. This noise was really

---

[18] In the Celtic cultures, the Bard/Filidh/Ollave was inviolate. He could travel anywhere, say anything, and perform when and where he pleased. The reason for this was, of course, that he was the bearer of news and the carrier of messages, and, if he was harmed, then nobody found out what was happening over the next hill. In addition, he carried the Custom of the country as memorized verses...he could be consulted in cases of Customary (Common) Law. He was, therefore, quite a valuable repository of cultural information, news, and entertainment.

alarming to hear, not knowing what it could be. My mind went through all kinds of scenarios wondering about that noise.

Later that night the storm came through. It was not just any storm but the tail end of that predicted hurricane. Our tent was blown apart and our gear was all over the place. Within an hour Monica and I were racing around gathering the children and stuffing our gear into the trunk.

Not to be dissuaded, the following weekend we went back and camped again. That evening we heard the sound we had heard the first time we camped. That long shrill call of something out on the pond. When we looked we saw a beautiful Loon in the moonlight and knew that what had frightened us was a Loon making its' night song. That night we listened to the ancient beautiful call of the Loon and found a new love for the beauty of that place. After that we would come back each spring to greet the Loons as they would return to their summer homes to have their babies and spend their summers. It became a dedication that I would look forward to all year long, as would my kids while they grew up.

It has not been unusual from that time for me to bring up my fondness for the Loon to anyone who would listen.

Over the years attending circle at Zhinquak's home we would talk about community and family as it relates to Native American teachings. I often would mention my families' love for the Loon. I would point out the Loons family qualities.

Whenever we were in circle and talking with the feather, I would always seem to have something lengthy to say. One night at the circle I finished speaking and passed the feather to Zhinquak. His first comment was that he could tell that I had to be Loon Clan.

That didn't make me Loon Clan, but I definitely was pleased to be recognized. In actuality, I don't think Zhinguak was relating the comment to some of the better attributes of the Loon, but that did not matter so much to me. That he inferred that I might be of the clan of my favorite bird was enough for me.

When I met Austin at the Midewiwin ceremonies, he had a tremendous impact on me. He seemed to know me better than I know myself in many ways. It was as if we had always known one another.

While at the Midewiwin ceremony, he asked me if I would come up to Barre, Canada the following April to a ceremony he was going to have. He explained it would be his twentieth year of sobriety and that he wanted all of the people in his circle to be there.

I felt very flattered that he would ask me and told him I would come. I remember thinking at the time that this was nice but more than probably just a nicety being given with no real intent that it would occur.

Not long after Zhiingwak had made the comment about me being Loon Clan I got a call from Austin.

"Booshoo, Jim, this is Austin. How are you?" Austin asked on the phone.

"Booshoo, Austin. I am great and how are you?" I answered.

"Oh. I'm good, aye. Just wanted to call to see if you are still going to come to my ceremony here in Barre in April?" Austin inquired.

"Well yes, I will try to get up there. What can I bring? I said.

"You don't have to bring anything. Just come. If you really want to bring something you could bring a large bag of tobacco. We can't get the large bags here in Canada, aye." Austin answered.

I answered; "Consider it done. Give me directions and I will be there."

"That's good, aye. I really am looking forward to seeing you. You will stay at our house." Austin responded.

This was fantastic! I knew I had really made a great friend and I couldn't wait to go. It would be good to meet the rest of Austin's family. I missed Austin and Pellie since the Midewiwin ceremonies and wondered if Austin would really call me to come to the ceremony at his home. Now he had.

April came around and I borrowed Monica's car to drive up. She had a Saab and it was more economical than my Jeep Cherokee. This was to be a fast trip up and back. It took about twelve hours to get there from New Hampshire.'

When I arrived Austin invited me into his home and introduced me to his wife, Kelly and little girl, Bailey. Everyone sat and talked for awhile and they made me feel right at home.

Austin was different than I had remembered him before. He was uptight and cranky. He was really stressed over something and I wanted to help in some way but I didn't know what I could do.

Kelly could see I was concerned and when Austin went out to the store she talked to me. "This is a very special ceremony", Kelly said. "Austin wants it to be just right and he is a little touchy right now but he will be okay."

Twenty years of sobriety is an important land mark, I thought. It is especially important when you are only around forty one years old and found sobriety at a younger age. I guess I could understand he might be nervous that it would come off well.

I helped where I could and Pellie came over from Christian Island where the Rez is located. Pellie was full of cheer and still always smiling. Aye?

The ceremony would be held at the Indian community center in downtown Barre, Canada. When I got there I felt a little out of it. Everybody was Indian and they all knew each other. Pellie, Kelly and Austin were all busy making sure everything was ready. They wouldn't let me do anything, so I kind of stood around not saying much to anybody.

I saw a few people that I recognized from the Midewiwin ceremonies. I didn't know them well enough to go up and make much conversation.

One of those people was Hector. Hector came over and said hello, but we didn't have much to talk about.

I looked over to the entrance door and suddenly there was someone standing there that I recognized. Standing in the door was Peter. A woman was standing next to him who must have been his wife, but I did not know for sure. Peter had not mentioned that he had a wife when we were at the ceremonies.

Peter walked over and smiled as he extended his hand and said, "Booshoo!"

"Boy! It is good to see you! I didn't know you would be here. Austin didn't tell me you were coming." I said.

"It was kind of a last minute thing to come. Lou and I didn't have anything else to do today. I don't know Austin real well and we weren't sure if we should come but decided that we would anyhow." Peter answered.

Peter continued; "This is my life partner, Lou. Peter gently motioned to the woman next to him."

"Booshoo, Lou. It is good to meet you." I said as she offered her hand and a traditional hug.

"Maybe", she said. "We'll see. I'm not Ojibwe you know? I am Oneida and we will see when I get to know you."

"OK!" I answered.

That is a different greeting, I thought. She seemed very genuine and obviously matter of fact. It would be interesting to see where this would go. It was not to go any further at that moment though. As soon as we were introduced she turned and went to the kitchen to help the women preparing the food.

"Peter, you have come a long way. You live on Six Nation Reserve south of Hamilton Canada don't you?" I asked.

"Yes", he said. "I live on New Credit Reservation next to Six Nation Reservation. We are the Ojibwe Mississauga of the New Credit. We were removed from the New Credit River in Toronto to that place in 1847.

It is only a few hours' drive and the weather is good. You came all the way from New Hampshire and that is a lot longer drive." Peter answered.

We both laughed.

"I brought something for you." Peter said.

He handed me a carved wooden spoon.

"It is beautifully made Peter. Did you make it?" I asked.

"Yes! I made two. One for you and one for Austin." Peter answered.

"Miigwich [thank you]." I responded.

The intercom music stopped and a powwow drum sounded four times. It indicated that the gathering was to begin. Austin had the mic and thanked everyone for coming. He handed the mic to an Elder who I had not seen before. The Elder began in his language and spoke for about five minutes offering the prayers for all of our relatives, Creator, and all of the people. He then welcomed the people and repeated the prayers in English so that everyone could relate to the prayers that were given.

The drum started after the opening ceremony and the place took on the feel of an indoor powwow. Everybody danced. There were probably a hundred people at the event. Austin was running around making sure everything was going smoothly and taking care of any problems that might arise.

I was very taken to have been invited to attend this event. I found Pellie, and asked him if I could do something special as a gift to honor Austin. I asked if I could bring in my flute and offer a song for Austin. Pellie told me to give the drum some tobacco and make the request.

At the break, Pellie went up and began to speak for his brother. He acknowledged all of the people who had come. He greeted each of his six brothers and two sisters. Then he told them that a special song was to be given to Austin and that the visiting chimookamon [chi-moo-ka-mon / long knife], long knife, from New Hampshire would play the flute.

I picked up my flute, said a prayer silently as I held the flute up. I began to play. The first note came out as a squeak and I stopped.

"That wasn't what I wanted to do," I said out loud. A few people chuckled.

I had only played in front of people once and that was as back up for White Crow.

When I began to play the flute gave off a loud squeal. I started again. This time the flute began to play. It was as if it were playing by itself. The song was beautiful and the notes were clear and flawless. As I heard it play I could not believe I was making the flute sound so beautiful. I know no songs and play what I feel in my heart trusting that Spirit will provide a song. This time it did!

I finished the song and Austin came out and thanked me for the gift.

Kelly came over to where I was standing and asked me if I would play the song again later so she could record it in memory of Austin's ceremony. I explained to her I could not because I don't know any songs and I would never be able to play it exactly the same again.

After the break, Austin and the Elder who opened the ceremony went to the center of the room. All of Austin's brothers and sisters came to the center and joined with Austin. Austin turned to the people and announced, "Will Noodin come to the drum".

My name was still new to me and I paid no attention until I realized that Austin's family was looking across the room at me. I walked to the center and noticed that Peter had gone to the Eastern direction of the circle and Hector had gone to the West.

The Elder started to speak in Ojibwe offering prayers. I thought it was the closing ceremony because I couldn't think of anything else that could be happening. The elder concluded and Austin took the mic and announced to the people. I want to introduce you to my brother, Noodin. He did this facing each of the directions.

I looked at Austin. I said to him in a low voice; "I didn't know you were going to do this."

"I recognized that you are my brother the first time we met, Noodin." Austin replied.

So much happened that year. I felt that I needed to do something more to understand the direction that I am traveling in life. I found Hector and asked him what I should do if I wanted to fast. Hector told me to contact him later and offer tobacco and he would see if he could help.

Everyone at the gathering then cleared the floor and brought out tables for the feast. And what a feast it was! There was Moose roast, Venison, Wild Rice, Berries of all kinds and many other dishes. So much food it could not possibly all be consumed by the people that were there.

The Moose roast was the best meat I ever tasted and it could be cut with a wooden spoon. Everything prepared was done in the native way. There were wild rice dishes, berries of all kinds, squash, fish and other things I really could not describe.

Later that evening, Austin and I gathered the leftover food and took it into the woods to bury. Feast meals are offered to Spirit and anything left should be offered back to the Spirits through mother earth. There was still about three feet of snow on the ground so it was a real task to dig and bury the food.

After burying the food ,Austin and I sat to talk. Pellie came in and joined us. First Austin told me that his eldest brother had died many years ago when Austin was young. It is a practice of the Ojibwe to adopt a person into families to take the physical presence of someone who has been lost too soon in life.

"You will be our eldest brother, aye? But remember", he said, "our eldest brother is just over in Spirit world and watching what you are doing so you better do everything right." Austin and Pellie laughed hard and long over that.

Austin explained to me that we are of Loon clan and told me several Loon legends for me to understand the importance of the clan. He told me that we are a chieftain clan, a story telling clan and also ambassadors of sorts.

Then Austin told me one of the clan legends about how Loon got his colors after helping the anishinabe, Indian. It is a beautiful story and I will tell it to you some time.

Noodin spoke to Misho; "I don't know Misho, but I don't believe it is a mistake that I am Loon Clan. Spirit has a way of making things happen when we allow it."

Misho responded; "There are many ways that Great Spirit lets us know who we are. He tells each of us these things. Many do not hear when Spirit speaks. That can be a blessing not to know. Often Spirit tells of things we would rather not know. Other times though, Spirit informs of gifts to help us in our lives as well as others who we meet.

Spirit speaks to you Noodin. Listen carefully and learn to hear the words. You will know the pain of knowing and the joy of knowing as well. Remember that the gift is for the people, and help where you can.

This is what family is about. We are all connected"

Misho left early the next morning to go to Pat Lillies for a visit. It was a short trip, and he would be back in Minnesota by the end of the week.

CHAPTER NINE

Fasting Time

~ *M'naa den d'mowin* ~ [respect] Respect everyone, all humans and all things created. Regard each with esteem and consideration. Allow others to believe in their own reality.

The mountain was heavily fogged in, and it was an overcast and drizzly day. Usually hikers that do come on days like that are experienced regular hikers that don't need to be monitored. Others who have little or no experience tend to wait for the sunny days. It is still a good idea to be prepared and check out some of the trails though.

Two days had passed since Misho's visit. Noodin was walking down to the park office to pick up a fresh radio and start up the mountain. As he looked down the road he saw a familiar red truck coming up the road. It was Misho.

"What is he doing back here?" Noodin wondered.

Misho got out of the truck and greeted Noodin. "Booshoo, Noodin, mino giizhigut [greetings wind, it is a good day.] Can we talk some more?"

"Sure." Noodin answered. "I have plenty of time since there aren't that many people coming to the mountain today."

"I'm not in a big hurry going back and wanted to visit a little more. Can we have a fire?" Misho said.

"I'll get a fire and some coffee started, Misho."

When the fire was set, Noodin poured Misho a cup of coffee.

Misho spoke; "Sometimes Noodin, I think we are living so far apart that I can't really help you as I should. You seem to have gained a lot of understanding from others when I am not here. Listening to you, I know that most of those things are very much the same things I would share with you. Are your brothers giving you some of the teachings to help you?"

Noodin spoke to Misho; "You are my teacher, Misho. You are the one that first said you would teach me and I learn from you. Things I learn from others I bring back to you to make sure they are correct as you understand them.

The reality is that I first began to learn from my Ojibwe brothers for five years before I learned my name, six years before I was adopted to a family. It had been nine years since I first read the book "Bury My Heart at Wounded Knee". Twenty one years had passed since I began sobriety in AA.

Even that amount of time no longer seemed to me to be when I began the walk on this road. There were other things I needed to know about myself that still were not clear. The more I learn from my red brothers the less, it seems, I know. That I know about the world, the people, the creation and even about myself."

"Yes." Misho commented, "You have always mentioned when others have shown you things. What do you do when you have no one to ask?"

"That happened to me a few years ago, Misho. I wanted to talk to you, but couldn't find you anywhere. I was feeling like I had reached a place where there was nowhere to go. It was time, Misho, for me to take another step. All of the things I was beginning to understand about walking this path were making me realize that I needed to do more. I realized that in reality the understanding I had gained was no more than an equivalent to about an eight year old in the teachings of the traditional Native American. It was time to ask for answers. But who to ask if I could not find you?

Peter often would talk of finding direction in his life to help the people and stay focused. He would tell me that he would fast every year or two for four days to be more at one and in balance with Creator and the creation.

I thought of something Austin had told me about Hector. That Hector puts people out on fasts and is one of Austin's elders."

Misho answered; "You mean Hector from the medicine lodge that lives in the eastern door? Over near Parry Sound, Ontario?

"Yes, I think you know him Misho." Noodin said.

"I do, he is a good man. Did he put you out?" Misho answered.

"I hoped that he would put me out so I called him. I figured that at least he might tell me what I should do." Noodin responded.

Phone to Hector from Noodin; "Hello!"

"Hector, this is Jim Beard. I need to talk to you for a minute if you have time."

"Sure Jim, go ahead."Hector answered.

"I need to go out on fast and I know that you put people out. Can you tell me what I should do?" I inquired.

"Do you want me to put you out?" Hector asked.

"If you would do that I would feel more comfortable doing it." I answered.

Hector asked; "Why do you need a fast Jim?"

"It is time Hector. I have learned things walking this way and the things I have learned make me feel I need to know more. I need direction from Spirit to know how to continue. People are asking me to help and Spirit is putting things in front of me. I feel I will better understand if I take some time to be at one with myself and Spirit." I answered.

"How long do you want to go out for, Noodin?" Hector asked.

"Four days and nights, I think." I said.

"I will be putting out some people in the spring. You need to begin to prepare for that time. I will let you know the exact time when we determine the date. You need to bring me tobacco for this, aye. Until then you are making preparation. You must not take any life between now and then. Do you understand?" Hector asked.

"Yes," I answered."

"I will get in touch with you sometime in March to let you know when we are going to go out. Aye?" Hector said.

"OK Hector. Thanks a lot, chi miigwich [chi me-gwitch / big thank you]. Ahow!" I said and hung up the phone.

I thought about the commitment I was making. The take no life statement made sense but I couldn't help but wonder why he made such a big point about it.

Every day when I would put out my tobacco offering, I would pray about the fast and the preparation.

Oshki had talked about fasting to me a few times. He even offered to put me out once. Oshki indicated that I would set up willow sticks in the four directions in a place out in the bush.

Peter and others had also talked about the things to do when out for fast. Some people said you could go out as a group and others said it is something you do alone.

For me, I felt it is something I need to do by myself. Austin and Hector seemed to agree, but noted that it is very important to have supporters that know you are out there and where you are. Just to make sure you are all right if for no other reason.

We were coming into spring that year. A lot was going on in my life at that time. Not the least was the progression of divorce proceedings. Yes, this was the time of executing the action of ending that withering marriage per my wife's desire. I had just received the notice the court proceedings would begin in April.

Several days after receiving this information I got a call from Hector. He informed me that the Fasting would start on the fourteenth of April, and I needed to meet him at Parry Island in Canada on the Reservation at that time.

"I can't make it!" I answered.

Misho asked somewhat alarmed, "You didn't go? After you offered your tobacco?"

"That was the response I got from Hector too." Noodin answered.

"There was a long silence on the other end of the phone when talking to Hector. I could imagine what he was thinking. Another wannabe!" Noodin added.

"What's going on Jim?" Hector asked.

"I am going through a divorce and the courts have notified me that I have to appear in April, Hector. I have to be in court." I answered.

"Can I come at a later time?" I asked.

Hector answered. "I will be putting people out in the fall and you could come then. That is a long time Noodin and you have committed to Spirit world for this. You have to continue your preparations through the summer. You cannot take any life until your fast is complete. You can't mow a lawn, pick medicines or do anything that might take life. That is a long time Jim. You understand that, aye?"

"Yes, I understand, Hector. I can do that." I responded.

"You have to be careful, Jim, while going through the court thing. Everything you do or say will be heard in Spirit world. The Spirits will wonder why you are keeping them waiting." Hector explained.

"You must do ceremony every morning and night. Do you have a pipe, Jim? Hector asked.

"Yes, I have a personal pipe, Hector." I replied.

"Then use the pipe everyday to offer your asema [a-same-a / tobacco]." Hector instructed.

"OK, Hector. I will do as you say." I said.

"You need to call your brother Austin and let him know. Your family is also making preparations for your fast and they will need to know you are not coming." Hector added.

"OK, Hector, I will call Austin right now." I answered.

"Good luck, Jim. I hope everything goes okay for you and your family through this time." Hector said.

"Thank you Hector. I appreciate that. I will be sending prayers for those that are fasting. I will talk to you again soon and let you know how things are going." I replied, and then hung up the phone.

The night before the first day of court, I had an anxiety attack. At least that is what I would call it. I had never had one before or since so I can only surmise it was an anxiety attack.

I was camped at a State Park just over the border into Massachusetts. Not far from Manchester, New Hampshire, where the court proceedings would start in the morning.

I never felt lonely when I camped and with all that was happening I was camping all of the time. On this night I felt truly alone and afraid. Just be calm and honest and everything will be all right I told myself.

I remembered what Hector told me about turning my pipe every day. I decided I would hold a circle by myself that night. I smudged the area around my camp and prepared the fire. Brought out my bundle and laid it in front of where I would sit in the west facing the fire and the eastern direction. My prayers were offered for the fire and I made a food offering from my mid day meal. I brought out my feathers and my pipe and smudged the pipe. As I said my opening prayers, I turned my pipe to the directions as I had been shown to do by Oshki.

I opened my eyes and looked across the fire. There were people standing all around. Not just a few but many people all around the circle and in back of one another back into the woods. They were wearing different kinds of clothing. Some wore regular street clothes, others were in Indian clothing and others wore suits. They stood around the fire watching me.

I blinked to see if this apparition would disappear. It didn't! The people just stood there, waiting. I only spoke in Ojibwe the best I was able. Slowly and deliberately I spoke the things I wanted to say to all of these people.

I told them the legend of the creation. Said prayers for all of them in Ojibwe the best I could.

After the legend, I spoke of what was happening and asked for their support as my family and I went through this time.

I was quiet for a time and more comfortable. As I looked around they were still all standing there. Just watching and waiting.

Then I picked up my flute and played songs for them for a long time.

I picked up my drum and began to sing a song of thanksgiving:

Gi zhi Manidoo	Great Spirit
Gana wa ba ne	We see you
Anishi na be	We people
Miigwich Manidoo	Thank you Spirit
Hey ya hey ya hey	
Hey ya hey ya hoo	
Gi zhi Manidoo	Great Spirit
De we igon	For the Drum
Anishi na be	We people
Miigwich Manidoo	Thank you Spirit
Hey ya hey ya hey	
Hey ya hey ya hoo	
Gi zhi Manidoo	Great Spirit
Maa doo di swan	For the Sweat Lodge
Anishinabe	We people
Miigwich Manidoo	Thank you Spirit
Hey ya hey ya hey	
Hey ya hey ya hoo	

Gi zhi Manidoo	Great Spirit
Bi madi zi win	For Life
Anishi na be	We People
Miigwich Manidoo	Thank you Spirit
Hey ya hey ya hey	
Hey ya hey ya hoo	

Hey ya hey ya hey
Hey ya hey ya hoo
Hey ya hey ya hey
Hey ya hey ya hoooo

I closed the ceremony to all of the directions, and the people waited. I then turned my pipe and separated it. When I looked up, the people were gone. Only the quiet and beauty of the forest in the darkness of night with the light of the fire remained.

I put the pipe down next to me and fell asleep there at the fire. I didn't wake until morning. When I awoke I felt refreshed and ready for the day before me.

Thank you, Creator, I said out loud.

The court hearings lasted about four days and then everything was put in the hands of the judge. I was told it might be three or four months before we would get a ruling. The sting of the proceedings was painful but Monica and I were still able to remain civil with one another and look to the interest of our kids, Stephanie and Nicholas.

We didn't hear anything more on the Judge's ruling until late October, so things were somewhat apprehensive through the summer.

In September I got another call from Hector. We are going to fast on October 10th Noodin. Are you ready?"

"Yes, Hector. I will be there!" I answered

I called Austin and told him that I was coming. He told me to get there a couple of days early and stop at his house. "We have things to do," he said.

I drove out of New Hampshire and it was a beautiful day. Mino giizhigut, I thought. It is a good day! The border traffic was light and the Canadian border patrol just kind of glanced at me and said, go ahead.

Along the way I stopped at Peters' and did lodge with him in preparation for the fast. It was a short stop and we did not have time to visit because I needed to get to Austin's' place."

Misho said; "You do a lot of lodges at Peter's when you travel that way don't you."

Noodin answered, "Yes! Almost every time. He is a good name sponsor and brother to me."

Noodin continued. "When I arrived at Austin's we had dinner and visited before going to bed".

"Was it a good trip?" Asked Kelly.

"Yes, it didn't take as long as usual and the traffic was light." I answered.

"We have a lot to do tomorrow." Austin said. "We have to pick up Pellie at the ferry launch in Midland so that he can help. Then we have to gather some things you will need. We ought to get some sleep, aye?"

"Okay", I said, and we all turned in for the night.

In the morning, Austin and I drove up to Midland to pick up Pellie. When we met him he was smiling as always. He had lost a lot of weight and looked a lot different. When he smiled he had all of his teeth for one thing.

"I have Diabetes," he said. "It is okay though aye. I am doing everything the doctors tell me."

"I also pledged for the Midewiwin, Noodin. I need to go to all of the ceremonies before I can initiate."

"That is great, Pellie." I said. He really looked good and it was good to see that he was taking care of himself.

We drove away from the ferry launch and up the road a short distance and Austin told me to pull up to the side of the road. We were next to a forest of very old White Cedar.

"We need to gather some cedar for your fast, Noodin", Pellie commented as he got out of the car.

We gathered enough cedar to line a circle. Probably about a bushel.

When we returned to Austin's home, Austin went into the garage and brought out a canvas tarp. It weighed about 50lbs.

"This will give you good cover from the cold." Austin said. "Do you have a plastic tarp about 6' by 6'?"

"Yes! In the car. I also brought plenty of twine and my axe." I said.

"We will need those things too." Said Austin.

The next morning Pellie, Austin and I got into the car.

"Why are you going with me?" I asked. "Aren't I supposed to do this alone?"

"You will! You will, aye! We will be your family of supporters. You will see." Pellie laughed as he told me these things.

We arrived in Parry Sound and crossed the bridge onto the Rez. As we drove along, we spotted an old red pickup truck with some boys sitting in the back. The truck turned onto a dirt road from the main road going through the Rez.

"Follow that truck, Noodin. That is Hector." Austin said.

I followed the truck for a couple of miles into the bush. The truck pulled up to a stop, and we stopped behind them. Everybody got out. Hector greeted us and introduced the other four people with him. His son Waz, a young man named Terry, another young man named Sam and a boy named Biindigen. They would be fasting too, Hector explained.

Hector instructed us to ask for saplings from a grandfather maple and take a certain number of saplings for our shelters.

"Don't we use willows for this?" I asked.

"We do when we can but the willows are pretty well cleaned out around here so we will use maple saplings." Hector explained.

We gathered the saplings and Hector instructed us to lay them on the ground. He told us to get in the vehicles and we would go back to his house to get ready to start the fast.

"There will be two girls fasting out here too, aye." Hector told us. "They are entering womanhood and this is the coming out for them."

When we got to Hectors house we sat down and had a ceremony at the fire. Hector explained that we would be fasting for four days. The fire will continue for the whole time you are fasting. Each night your families will come out and sing for you nearby. I will be around now and then to see that everyone is ok. You will not see me and I will not interrupt your fast. You do not leave your fast spot for any reason except to go to the bathroom.

Then we had a meal. All the Kentucky Fried Chicken and pizza you could eat.

We drove back to the place on the road where we left the saplings. Each of the people fasting gathered the saplings and cover and Hector told us to go into the woods and select spots well apart from one another to make our fasting place.

Hector, Pellie and Austin came around and helped me to put up my shelter.

"In spring we don't use shelters." Pellie said. "Now it is cold and the weather can be pretty bad so we will make shelters."

The construction of the lodge is similar to the sweat lodge in the placing of the poles in the ground and the lodge is just big enough for the person to lay down head to toe to the edge of the lodge. An inner line was tied from pole to pole. The plastic tarp was put down as a floor and wrapped over the inner line. The tarp that Austin let me use was then laid over the lodge for a cover with just enough of an opening to get in and out. Then a cedar line was laid all the way around the lodge about a foot out from the structure itself. The finished lodge was 6' in diameter and 3' high. Just large enough so that I could have shelter.

A small supply of kindling had been gathered and I put that inside the lodge to keep it dry. After the fasting spot was prepared we all met back on the road and had a circle. We smudged and each offered our prayers.

Hector gave the final instructions. "You need to light a small fire and offer your tobacco at dusk and at dawn and around noon each day. Have all of your medicines; tobacco, sweat grass, sage and cedar and offer those to the fire each time with your prayers. If you feel that you have to leave the fast then come out quietly so as not to disturb the others who are fasting and wait at the road. Someone will come by and you can get a ride back to my house."

We all left and went to our fasting spots.

I crawled in and looked around. Then I made a small fire at the entrance and offered my medicines.

It was cold, around 30 degrees, so I stayed bundled and tried to meditate for awhile. After a time I felt really tired and laid down to sleep. The sleep only lasted for what seemed an hour or so and I woke because my hips were sore from lying on the ground. I went out by the lodge and inside the cedar line for awhile to stretch. I was getting hungry and it was getting dark.

I went into the lodge and fell asleep for an hour or so. When I woke up it was pitch black. I lit my fire and made an offering. I went in the lodge and prayed until I fell asleep again.

Later, I thought I heard singing in the woods. It was singing! The people had come out to the edge of the fasting area and were singing songs to us of prayer to help us in our fast. It was beautiful to listen to and I didn't want it to stop. After awhile it was quiet again and the people had gone away.

The more time that went by the more tired I became. Dehydration, I decided, was making me tired. Every time I would fall asleep I would wake up in an hour or so because of soreness and hunger.

After a time, I would wake up and realize that I had been dreaming. I couldn't make out the dreams. They were grayish and shadowy. I kept wanting to have some great inspiration come to me, but nothing would come.

It rained all night, and I was cold and uncomfortable. When daylight came, I lit my fire and made my offerings, then went back to sleep.

The weather cleared up for a couple of hours in the morning and I saw a starling fly through the woods and right past me. From east to west he flew. I thought to myself, what could that mean? Probably nothing!

The evening was the same, and the rain started again. It got colder and I was hungry. My stomach ached for food and a drink of water. I kept having grayish dreams that I could not remember, and the end of the fourth day was coming. At least I had really done a fast, I thought.

Not everyone has some great experience but fasting is supposed to be an offering of yourself for the people. I was doing that and tried to keep my prayers focused on that.

I heard a crackling of footsteps in the woods. It was Bill, one of Hectors' helpers.

It is time for you to break down your lodge, Noodin. Fold up your things and tie the poles together in a bundle to take out. Hector will be by in a few minutes to release you from your fasting place.

I came out and made my fire to offer the rest of my medicines. I collected the cedar line and offered that to the fire as well.

I brought down the tarp and folded it neatly so that it would be easier to carry. Each pole had to be untied and then the bundle of poles was tied together with the twine I had used to tie the individual poles.

As this work was being done, I stopped for a moment to look around. The sun had come out and it was a beautiful day. As I looked to the west I could feel a soft breeze in my face and it felt clean and fresh.

I stood there looking out and the wind began to shift. The wind blowing from the west started moving around me. It shifted to the north, to the east, the south and back to the west. That is odd I thought. I don't remember the wind going all the way around me like that before.

Hector appeared from behind me. I didn't hear him at all until he spoke.

"Are you okay, Noodin?" He asked.

"Yes, I am good." I answered.

Hector handed me a quart size bottle of yellow looking liquid. "What do I do with this?" I asked.

"Drink it. Drink it down as fast as you can. Drink every bit of it!" Hector said.

I took the bottle and drank it down. It was strong and didn't taste great. I drank it all and put the bottle down.

Immediately, I started to throw up.

Hector encouraged me; "Get rid of it. All of it!"

"Aaagh! What was that?!" I said.

"Cedar tea", Hector answered. "Now you have purged and everything in you has been cleansed. Take your things down by the cars and I will meet you there."

"Hector," I said, "Thank you for all you have done. I cannot believe how kind you all have been to me."

"We are a loving people, Noodin. "He answered."

When Hector got to the car, we all gathered together. We six who fasted awaited our instructions.

Hector gave instruction, "Noodin, take everyone who fasted in your car and follow me. I want you to park in a place where no one will see you and wait for me to come and get you.

I will bring you all into the community house and you will wait in the hallway. You will hear the people singing a welcoming song beckoning you to return to them. Be hesitant and peek in now and then but act like you aren't sure that you want to return. Then, reluctantly, begin to dance in to your places in the front of the circle."

Everybody's got it, aye?"

We all said yes and followed Hectors car to the community center.

There were cars all over the place. The center was jammed with people. We stayed in our car behind a garage next to another car that held the two girls who had fasted.

Hector and a Grandmother who was caring for the girls came out and led us all into the hallway. We waited and the people began to sing. The song they were singing was a traveling song to invite us to come in and join with them. It seemed as though I had never heard such a beautiful song. It sounded like spirits singing as I listened.

We did as Hector had told us and acted as if we did not want to return but wished to stay in spirit world. Then we danced in to our places at the front of the circle.

Prayers were offered, more songs were sung, and a pipe was lit and passed around.

A lady stood and asked to speak. Everyone was quiet to give her the floor.

She made a statement; "I am a Christian and do not trust these things that you are doing. My grandson insisted he must do this and it is the only reason I am here. I pray for forgiveness of all of you and that my grandson comes to his senses. What you are doing is worshiping the devil and can only bring harm."

She sounded very bitter as she ostracized all of the people. She said a few more things and then excused herself and left the gathering. No one said anything further about the incident.

Each of us who fasted was asked to stand before the people and tell them of our experience. First was Waz, Hectors son, and then me and the others.

I felt lacking as the others spoke of their fast. They had experienced dreams and answers to questions. One had a bear come by his lodge and climb a tree next to him for the night.

I had nothing! I introduced myself; "Booshoo. Noodin indizhinikas, Maang indodem, Zhaganaashi indow. [Greetings, Wind is how I am known, Loon is my clan, I am English.]"

As I spoke I mentioned what little I could and what a wonderful experience it had been. I used as much Ojibwe language as I could to honor the people that were there.

Then I got to the place where I was gathering my things. I told them of the wind, "I stood there looking out and the wind began to shift. The wind blowing from the west started moving around me. It shifted to the north, to the east, the south and back to the west. "

I heard some of the elders saying aho, howaa and other explanations of being impressed. Why was that a big deal? I wondered.

After we spoke the feast meal was uncovered. Each of us was brought a meal by a woman of our clan. A mother, wife or sister. In my case a midewiwin woman acted as my family to serve me.

When she brought me my meal I said; "Gowiin [gow ween, no], feed my grandmother first. " She brought me a second meal and I answered; "Gowiin, no, feed the children first." She brought me a third meal and I said; "Gowiin, no, feed the people first." The fourth meal was brought to me and I said; "Miigwich, thank you, and accepted the meal." This was part of the tradition of acceptance and giving of the people.

After the meal was a gifting, and a large blanket was put out on the floor. All of the gifts we had brought were on the blanket and everyone went up to take a gift from the eldest down to the youngest of the children.

This was the ending of the ceremony and the fast. After some time socializing with the people it was time to leave.

As Pellie, Austin and I drove back to Austin's house I asked Austin. "Why did the elders make comments when I told my experience in the fast? Nothing really notable happened for me."

Austin answered;"Noodin, don't you know what happened? The wind coming in and circling you that way. Spirit acknowledged you and who you are. You are Noodin, Wind."

It was several years later while at a medicine ceremony in Wisconsin I came to realize more of the teaching of that fast. I was telling Pallah, my friend, about that night before my court date. In the telling I suddenly realized what had happened.

When I could not make it on the planned time I was supposed to fast. The time I had put my tobacco out for this offering to fast for the people. The time the Spirits knew I was to come. The time Hector told me the Spirits would be looking for me. That is the time that my fast actually began. How could that be?

When I was not there in Canada, but was camping in Massachusetts the night before my court appearance and I had a circle. It was the Spirits of my ancestors, supporters and helpers standing in that circle. They were there with me and helping me to go through that time.

They knew!

Misho spoke; "Truth is never evident in total. There is always more than we come to know. You are right, Noodin. They do know!"

CHAPTER TEN

Understanding the Signs

~ **Mashkode bizhiki** ~ [buffalo] Buffalo instructed Weno Booshoo, first man, that he should be respectful when he would meet his father.

By mid afternoon it was pouring rain. The wind was howling outside and tree branches were falling all around the cabin. The fire inside was warm. Gusts of wind were coming down the chimney and blowing smoke back into the room now and then, but the chimney would seem to take a deep breath and suck the smoke right back out again after about a minute.

Misho said; "It looks like I will be your guest for another night, Noodin."

"That is my honor, Misho. Glad to have you here."

"You know that everything is in front of you for you to make choices and that it is up to you to do what is shown don't you, Noodin."

"Yes, Misho, I understand that." Noodin answered.

"So how do you know when those signs are there? Have you learned to see what is being given?" Misho asked.

"Slowly I am coming to understand, Misho. I learn as I pay attention to what is around me." Noodin answered.

Noodin explained to Misho; "There was a time in New Hampshire. It was in the early fall. How beautiful it is at that time. I was preparing to drive to the ceremonies in Wisconsin and the temperature in the New England area was a moderate 56 degrees.

I had arranged to pick up my brother who is a member of the Medicine Society, Pellie, at our brother Austin's home in Barre, Canada. Pellie would be waiting in Barre. The drive from New Hampshire travels down to Massachusetts, then to New York State and then to the border at Niagara Falls. From the border you travel to Toronto and up the 407 highway to the 400 highway and then north. The total drive takes about twelve hours under normal conditions.

This was a special time for Pellie. It might be the last time he would be able to come to the States for ceremony because of his need for dialysis every two days to treat his diabetes. It was very important to me to be able to help my brother.

The drive was beautiful through New York and into Canada until I started north from Toronto. It started to snow and soon the roads were covered with snow and ice and the blowing wind created white out conditions. Even in stop and go traffic I sometimes could not see the car three feet in front of me. The storm continued through the night and it took several hours to travel around sixty miles up the highway. Cars and trucks were piled up everywhere and all I could do was carefully wind around them, hoping not to get hit or hit something myself. The storm continued as I reached Barre. It seemed unusual to hit a powerful snowstorm at this time of year.

I arrived in Barre at about 2 o'clock in the morning, and did not want to wake Austin and Pellie by knocking on the door in the middle of the night.. I pulled up at a truck stop near Austin's home and slept there in the car until about six o'clock. The storm continued, and I would wake up and run the car to keep enough heat so I wouldn't freeze.

Pellie and Austin were waiting when I arrived and we went back to the truck stop for breakfast. After breakfast Pellie loaded his gear into the Jeep and we started on our trip to the Medicine Ceremonies in Wisconsin.

Pellie and I continued from Barre north to Parry sound. At Parry sound, we turned west and began our trek toward Sault Ste. Marie. It was not long before we came into another snowstorm and more whiteout conditions. The storm continued all the way to the border at Sault Ste. Marie.

Just as we started to enter Sault Ste. Marie, the weather cleared. We crossed the border into Michigan and continued west toward Wisconsin.

As we drove away from the Sault, we saw a beautiful site to our north direction. It was the Aurora Borealis appearing in the sky. We could not help but stop the Jeep to watch the beautiful display of purple, green and yellow veils in the sky. We got out of the car and walked into a field to be able to fully take in this beautiful gift we were seeing. It was something I hadn't seen since I was a boy living in western New York. We stood there in awe as we watched the varied curtains moving about in different colors.

After a few minutes we got back in the car and proceeded down the Highway. A few minutes after starting our drive again, we ran into another snowstorm. The white outs were worse than before and we had to slow down and watch the path on the road in order to be able to continue.

After traveling about forty miles in whiteout conditions, at a speed of maybe fifteen miles per hour, the weather finally cleared and stars were showing.

Just before the weather began to clear, a White Wolf ran across the road in front of our car. It was a beautiful animal and gave us the sense that this road would be clear now. We had seen a sign!

To the Indian, animals do not just appear by coincidence but are often there to signify something that is happening or will happen. The Wolf is a protector of his family, a scout watching for dangers and hunting for food, and a messenger of wisdom.

It was no coincidence that the White Wolf crossed our path. I commented to Pellie: "I guess the road is going to clear up now, right?" He answered that it would.

A few miles down the road we cited another Wolf. This one was a large gray wolf that stood by the road as we passed by. Pellie and I both knew we would have a clean road for the rest of our trip to Bad River Reservation in Wisconsin, and it was. After all, we had seen the signs. We arrived at the Bad River Lodge at about three o'clock in the morning.

Early Tuesday morning Pellie and I drove to the school being built by the Ojibwe Medicine Society. When we arrived there, they had not begun to build the lodge for the ceremonies. There were a few workers there beginning to build an addition to the main building. We went up and became helpers to make the work go faster. It took two days to build the addition on to the main building, using three carpenters and two helpers. It needed to be completed so the building could be used as an entry area for ceremonies. While we were building the addition, other people from the nation were arriving and beginning to build the ceremony lodge. Work on the lodge lasted until midnight on Wednesday, and by that time everything was ready for ceremonies.

Ceremonies began with a sunrise ceremony early Thursday morning. After the Sunrise Ceremony were teachings given by Eddie Benton Banai, the Ojibwe Grand Chief of the medicine lodge. Most of the first teachings were given in preparation for the ceremonies to follow. Much of the direction was in reference to the new school to be built. The school being built by the three fires society is intended to teach young Indians in a traditional way and to give them an understanding of the Ojibwe language. The school is being built through donations from people, of materials and manpower. Building the school in this way is a long process and it is amazing when we think that three years ago this was only a dream.

All meals at ceremony are sacred feasts. Different feast meals are assigned to different Clans of the people. One feast may be provided by the Eagle Clan, the next one by Loon Clan and so on. The feast food is prepared by the women using a kitchen on the reservation at the community center. The men bring the food up for the feast to the ceremonies by van. The food is then blessed with a ceremony of thanksgiving and distributed to the people by the Clan that prepared the food. This is done with each meal for the four days of ceremony. In this way everyone is given an opportunity to help everyone else, by making sure that everyone has been fed.

All through the day, ceremonies and teachings are given to the people by the Elders and Chiefs of the medicine society. These ceremonies and teachings are offered in the traditional way of the people as has been passed down through generations.

Wherever the people decide to have their ceremony is a special place. It is a place I choose to be in. I learned from these people a special way to understand Creator and all creation. They believe in the Spirits of nature and of all life here, before and after and they teach me to understand the relationship of all things. Their teaching begins with the preparation of the grounds and construction of the lodges. I am grateful to be able to help them in this work.

Their ceremonies humbly honor all things and all life through prayer, music, dance and telling of legends of the people.

I feel honored to be able to participate when invited to do so. The Indian who follows a traditional way lives a spiritual life where each man or woman is considered one of many, and seeks to look out for the many.

One of the key factors of a ceremony is the ceremonial fire. The fire is a connection between Spirit world and the ceremonies of the people. It is critical that the fire be maintained and honored from the beginning of ceremony until the ceremony is ended. Fire keepers see to it that the ceremony fire continues to burn throughout the ceremony. The fire keeper is a member of the medicine society.

Sometimes the fire keepers have permitted me to sit at the fire and help them to care for it. This is a great honor for me, that they will trust me to maintain the fire when I'm not a part of the society. At this particular ceremony, I stayed with the fire for the last three nights. While keeping the fire during the nighttime, it is not unusual to have visitors. Sometimes an Elder would come by to honor the fire, and other times young people come by just to sit and to talk. When we talk about the traditional ways, the teachings we know and the legends we've been told, I always feel particularly blessed in that I walk away with new knowledge.

There's nothing magical about the fire. There's nothing magical about the ceremonies or about the Spirits. The beliefs of the Ojibwe have nothing to do with magic, superstition or mysticism. They understand that there is one Creator, a Mystery created all things and the universe. They accept that all things have a relationship with everything else and with the Creator. They honor all of these things and look upon all of creation as being related to them. Their beliefs lead them to show respect for all things. Their ceremonies, medicines and daily living ask for the honoring of Spirit in all life, and all things created by the Creator. Traditional people do not wish to convert others to follow their ways. Unlike many, they do not presume to be the authority of the Creator by the charge of what is right and wrong. They respect everyone's right to make a choice and they understand that there are many roads to the Creator. In the circle of life, it is said that whatever you do will come back to you, so the traditional teachings tell the people to walk a good path and to respect all life and all beliefs.

I am not trying to paint a picture of the Indian as a perfect being. The two leggeds who are Indian are human beings. Like all of us, they can make mistakes. When people follow the traditional way they try to walk in a manner that honors Creator and all things of creation. They understand that to have a good life is to walk in balance with themselves and with all things. In doing this, they strive to honor the generations that preceded them, while preparing a way for the generations to come.

The shortsighted accomplishments of our dominant society, and the rules today, are likely to be a threat to our future generations. The people who walk the, so called, red road in the traditional way hope that others will choose to honor the Creator and Mother Earth, as they do. They strive to set an example, hoping others will follow.

No ceremony passes where there isn't something revealed to change understanding, and the course of my life. It seemed like everything at this ceremony I was hearing had to do with the caring for the people.

It was the fourth night of the ceremony at around eleven thirty.

Though I have been attending ceremonies for a few years, there were still many native people who would basically be cordial, but distant. Especially the women of the tribe. An Anglo stands out in this population and the people have become leery of visitors to their sacred ceremonies.

To my surprise, a young woman in her early twenties walked up to me as I stood near the lodge listening to the teachings being given inside. "Excuse me", she said, "I want to ask if you could help me. I need a ride back to my motel." She looked down at her son, who was about four, and continued. "We have been here since six thirty this morning and my grandmother is in the lodge right now. It looks like it will be going on for a long time and my son is exhausted." I answered that I would be happy to give her a ride.

I could not help but feel honored that a woman of the people would trust me. It must have taken a lot of courage for her to even ask.

When we got in the car she commented to me, "I am thinking of leaving the lodge!"

I thought about what she had said. Why is she telling me, an outsider, this, that she would be thinking of leaving the lodge.

"Why would you want to leave the lodge?" I asked.

"I don't want to, but my aunties on my rez are all Christian and they are always after me about my beliefs. They tell me I am a pagan and devil worshiper. That I will go to hell if I do not change my ways. I am tired of their constant criticisms and if I leave the lodge they will get off my back." She replied.

I answered. "I really don't know what I can tell you to help. I am not a member of the Medicine Society and can't be since I am not an Indian. I guess all I can tell you is why I, a white man, would come to these ceremonies."

I told her how I had come to be invited to ceremony a few years ago. I spoke about how my brothers, Austin and Pellie, befriended me and began to share teachings that changed my life. How each time I come and help, I feel re energized and whole with myself. What I had learned about myself and where I came from, so as to understand where I am going in this lifetime and on. How I learned to laugh.

When I finished she said to me; "You have helped me see that this is my path. I am going to stay in the Midewiwin Lodge and I now understand why this is so important for me and my son. You know, it really is special how Creator puts signs on our road to help us when we need it."

"Yes", I answered. "This trip seems to be all about seeing the signs. On the way here, Pellie, my brother, and I went through several white out snow storms. When it looked like it could only get worse, we saw a white wolf run across the road in front of our car. We both knew the road would clear up after that and it did. Then, a little further down the road, we saw a grey wolf on the side of the road, watching us pass. We knew then that the road would stay dry for the rest of the trip. I never would have accepted that a few years ago. Today I know that Creator works with each of us in mysterious ways."

There was dead silence in the car and I looked at her. Her face was aghast as she looked at me. I asked; "What is the matter? Are you okay?"

She answered slowly and with deep reverence, "My son is White Wolf and I am Grey Wolf."

Nothing more was said until we arrived at her motel, some fifty miles from the Rez. We both knew something very profound had happened, and it was not a coincidence I was the one to give her a ride to her motel. She said good night and that she would see me in the morning at the lodge. She told me she wanted me to meet all of her family at ceremony in the morning.

Wolf has many teachings. He is brother to man and was the companion to the first man, Wena Booshoo, when he was put here by Creator. Wolf is a Clan of the people and people of the Wolf Clan are protectors of the families, scouts of the area for protection and the finding of food and shelter. They look out for family and help to teach us how to honor our family and take care of the community.

"Misho", said Noodin "You once told me that I have four animal spirit guides, and they might reveal themselves to me at some point in my life. The animals that were given in the four directions would be joined by these spirit guides and they would reveal themselves to me when I was ready to know them. I realized that the first of my guides had shown himself to be wolf. I came to understand that wolf would stand in my eastern direction to help me help others of my family. Wolf has shown me that I am family to my Indian brothers and sisters. It was a powerful teaching."

Misho answered; "We are all family, Noodin. You should know that."

"I do, Misho. It is special when you feel that connection." Noodin answered.

CHAPTER ELEVEN

Being a Helper

~ *Zaa gidwin* ~ [love] **The** love of life and creation that is felt by a seed planted as it senses the warmth of the soil heated by the sun. As it grows it pushes to the light and reaches out to feel the light and warmth. It honors the gift as it opens the petals of the flower to receive the bounties of life. It shares the bounties with all brothers and sisters that have need. Know this love and share it with all.

Misho's return visit was a special time. Noodin and Misho spent most of the day by the fire, looking out into the heavy fog that rolled through the forest. The night was quiet and peaceful. An Owl would call out now and then and one could hear distant responses from other Owl's far out in the forest. With the fog, it made the evening forest seem enchanted. Spirit seemed to be everywhere.

By morning, Noodin woke up as the sun rays came into the cabin. Misho was already up and outside doing his morning ceremony. Noodin joined him by the fire and made a morning offering.

"Pat Lillie told me that there are some people around New England who say they are medicine men, Noodin. Have you met any of them?"

"As I continue to walk on this road, I meet many medicine men but few true medicine men of the people. That is not to say that we as people do not carry the ability to heal ourselves and others, because I believe we all do. It is to point out that some people want the status, without an understanding of what they are really doing.

Some have names with medicine in the name to indicate they are medicine people, others claim to have powers to heal, and others assume that carrying certain sacred items gives them the power of a medicine man."

Misho speaks, "Not everyone who claims to be a medicine man truly is, Noodin."

"To me", Noodin answered, "a medicine man is known by the ability he exhibits, in the way he walks his path, the Elders that have passed on teachings to him and the effort he has applied to connect with the natural universal forces that aid in healing. He is a man that opens himself to Spirit, to allow Spirit to use him as a helper. He is a man or woman who helps an individual heal from within. The attention is given to applying the healing to all parts of man; emotional, physical, spiritual and mental.

I have seldom heard a true medicine man make the claim that he is a medicine man."

Misho replied; "That is a good way of seeing it."

Noodin went on; "Before beginning this walk, I didn't really believe in medicine people. I would see ministers of different religions healing, and then discover that much of what they claimed was false. People who did get better seemed so willing to believe, that the work of the medicine person almost seemed like a placebo, within their healing more psychosomatic than due to power of the medicine person.

I heard of some people among the Ojibwe and other aboriginal peoples who truly were said to be medicine people, and they were highly recognized for their ability to heal. The Ojibwe people are well known as a people who carry the medicines.

One such man of the Ojibwe is your son, Misho. He told me this about himself.

He told me that when he was a very young child, it was recognized that he had very special gifts. He is known, as Nish Nung, Two Stars, and was raised in the woods by his grandfather, a great Elder and a well known healer of the people. Under his guidance Nish Nung learned the teachings of the medicine people. He spent much of his childhood time with his grandfather and was tested and taught in the old ways. He was taught what are known as the traditional ways of the people.

He told me during his teenage years he was as rough as they come in the rez world, and it may have appeared doubtful that he would ever utilize his teachings to help the people. For that matter, it was doubtful if he would even make it to middle age. In time he did come to a place where he would pick up his sacred items and walk on the red road.

There came a time when he felt a need to be away from his home in Minnesota and traveled to New Hampshire. He was hoping to live with his adopted brother, Oshki, and to find work. Finding work was difficult. Just looking like an Indian is enough to turn many people away from hiring. Living at Oshki's was okay in the beginning for him but really did not lend itself to the kind of work that he wanted to do."

Misho responded; "is that when Nish Nung went to live at your place?"

"Yes, Misho" Noodin answered. "Nish Nung is an artist and he needed a place to do his painting while in New Hampshire. I had a well lighted cottage in Amherst, New Hampshire and invited him to come there to do his work. I soon found that he was there all of the time. He worked best late at night and would often stay over.

When we would talk, he would explain some of the medicine teachings to me and what he had experienced to learn medicine teachings of the people. He was also helpful in the language which I was struggling to understand better at that time.

One day Nish Nung commented that he really needed a ska be wis, [helper], to be with him when he is doing medicine healings. Someone to help prepare the medicines and to be present, so there would be no misunderstandings of intent by people who were present during the medicine work. It needed to be a person that understood enough to assist in ceremonies, and help to make things ready for work to be done.

I offered him my prayer tobacco and asked if I could be that helper. At the time I knew he might say no since I am not Indian and I know very little about medicines other than aspirin.

To my surprise and happiness, he said yes and accepted my tobacco prayer. This began an experience I can only equate to a college education about the people, the medicines, the teachings and the language. It was like an introduction to Creator and creation from a whole new perspective.

During this time, I would open the house for native circles almost weekly and we would have small gatherings. On occasion people would come to ask for help with illnesses they were suffering from. Nish Nung would never turn anyone away.

Misho asked; "How long did Nish Nung live at your place?"

"About two years, I think." Noodin answered.

"We traveled all over the USA and Canada during that time. It wasn't unusual to decide to go to see you in the afternoon, and get in the car and leave that night. We would drive straight through from New Hampshire to Minnesota and be at your place the next evening in time for dinner."

"Nish Nung would often work on his paintings at night, and it was normal for him to work until two or three in the morning. I, on the other hand, am one will go to bed around ten and get up at six. This worked well for us because we would both find some time to ourselves, a good thing in a small cabin. Nish Nung would sleep on the couch in the living room. I had the bedroom and spare room that I used for an office to myself. Another good thing for the two of us sharing the same space.

The only income that he had was from selling the paintings, which would sporadically bring in a few hundred dollars here and there. My funds were limited as well, after my divorce from my wife. Most of the assets went to her and I was basically starting over again. Being determined to walk this new path and to follow these new teachings did not exactly open up a fortune of new funds coming in. In fact, most of the work I was doing was offered at no cost, since the work involved sharing teachings that were freely given to me. During this time of two years, pretty much all of my assets would be exhausted. To subsidize the cash outflow, I would do carpentry and home repairs for friends. Nish Nung would often help with this work.

One day I received a call from a sister in my clan. Her name is Rebecca and her Indian name, Wabiigwan, means flower. Rebecca had known Nish Nung for many years and her teachings came from you, Misho, when you first began to travel to New England, back in the late eighties. When she heard that Nish Nung was back in New England and staying with me, she called to ask for help. She had Marie Strumpell disease[19] and many other illnesses had set in. Rebecca was disabled and living in an assisted living complex in Plymouth, New

---

[19] <u>Ankylosing Spondylitis</u> is a chronic inflammatory disease of the joints of the spine and those connecting to the spine, such as the sacroiliac joint. This is an arthritic condition involving stiffness in joints, with resultant pain and stiffness in the back and hips, and difficulty taking deep breaths, due to rib connection to spine.

Hampshire. When I told Nish Nung she had called, he replied that we should go there in the morning and visit her.

The next morning we drove the two hours from Amherst to Plymouth, New Hampshire to visit Rebecca. We found her sitting in a wheel chair in her two room flat. She could barely hold her head up to greet us when we came in. Her hands were malformed from the debilitating disease. It was hard to believe that at one time, not so many years ago, this woman had been astonishingly beautiful. She had even been featured in Playboy magazine in the mid seventies.

Nish Nung started asking her questions. She responded with information pertaining to her illnesses and also experiences in her life walk that might reflect reasons for the illnesses inflicted.

Nish Nung asked me to go to the car and bring in his bag with his medicines and pipe.

I was glad to go out and get those things. It was difficult to stay in there with this person who was so very Ill.

When I returned, Rebecca was lying on the bed and waiting for Nish Nung to begin his work.

I smudged the room and all of us. This would set up a protection boundary and invite Spirits to come help in the ceremony. Then Nish Nung took out his pipe and lit it. He offered prayers in Ojibwe for Rebecca and all people who suffer from sickness.

Nish Nung told me to take my drum and to begin drumming. "Don't stop drumming until I am finished," he said.

I began to drum as Nish Nung took out medicine stones and gave them to Rebecca with instruction to hold them as he continued.

He took a bald eagle feather and began to pass the feather over her as if he were searching for something. He would chant as he did this, and now and then he would stop in certain places and concentrate on particular areas of her body.

When he finished, I stopped the drum. We sat there while Rebecca got back into her wheel chair.

She seemed calmer than before and moved a little easier.

Nish Nung reached into his bag and took out a root he was carrying with him. He gave it to me and instructed me to grind it into a fine grain.

He boiled a cup of water, took a pinch of the root and put it into the water. He handed it to Rebecca. "Drink this", he said. "Drink a cup of this everyday and it will work to make you well."

Nish Nung then reached in his bag and took out a bottle that contained a salve. He asked Rebecca for a silver spoon and used it to take a spoonful of the salve from the bottle. He put it in a small glass for her. Nish Nung then said, "Put this on your hands every day. It will last a long time and it doesn't take much. It will relieve the pain in your hands and give you use of them again."

As I understand it, the work I witnessed is the old way of the people. The traditional way of people that have guided me to a limited understanding of Spirit and the Creator. At the time of this writing, many years past, Rebecca tells me she still has no pain in her hands. The overall treatment did not cure her of Marie Strumpell disease but it did relieve her of much of the pain, and many of the side related illnesses have gone away.

Nish Nung did what I have now seen many Elders do. He listened to Rebecca as she told him of the illness and the symptoms that she could relate to. Then he cleansed the area with medicine to alert the Spirits that a healing ceremony would begin.

We then cleansed ourselves with the medicine. Prayers of healing of the cause of the illness were offered and the Spirits were alerted by the drum that healing was being done. Everything that was done addressed the emotional, physical, spiritual and mental aspect of the person being worked on. It was a beautiful thing to see.

In the time I traveled with my brother, Nish Nung, I have seen these healings done many times. The work done is offered with love and respect for all things. Nothing is ever asked of the people asking for a healing. Gifting by them is accepted as an honoring of one another.

I once asked Nish Nung a question about doctoring as we drove across the country someplace in Wyoming.

I asked; "Nish Nung. How do you think these healings work? I mean, how do you know how you affect healings through spirit and ceremony? How it works?"

Nish Nung answered; "I do not really know. I can only tell you that as I use the feather or other tools and pray, I feel a sense of direction from Spirit that tells me what is wrong and guides me as to what to do. I trust in the guidance of Spirit. As for the medicines I use, they are passed down from Elders who carry that knowledge from generation to generation. It is not me; it is Spirit that does the work.

Using the medicines without the aid of Spirit can often be healing because the medicines carry their own healing properties. Using the medicines with the aid of Spirit will do more, because the healing is directed to the specific illness of that person seeking the healing. As the medicines are made, they are prayed for and Spirit is asked to direct the healing specifically for the person to be healed."

His answer was enlightening to me because I could feel the truth in what he had to tell me.

I believe one of the most common medicines of the people is community. When people work and live together they lend to one another that strength of community. The energy of one lends to the energies of many to give a healthy wholesomeness to the people of the community. Often, when you ask an Indian who he is, he will simply reply; I am one of many. He refers to that strength of his being one with the community.

A segment of that strength of the community is ceremony. It is a way of continuance of the healing of the people. One ceremony utilized on a continuing basis is the ceremony of circle. Whenever anything would be discussed, a circle would gather of the people to determine how to solve varied issues within the community. It might be as simple as when a hunting party would go out and where they would go. It could also be as detailed as moving a village to a new location. Circles would occur when Elders would sit to tell the at'i zookan [stories of the people] in order to pass on the oral teachings of the generations being carried on.

Another aspect of the circle is the sharing of information and the individual healing of people within a group, utilizing the strength of communicating with Spirit and each other. Often some item such as a feather, a rock, a stick or something else will be utilized. The item will be held by the leader or guide of the circle who will indicate that all of the people in the circle are the same. No one is above or below another. We are all people amongst the life of creation. The guide will then explain that the item being used is a talking item. The one holding the item is the only one who can speak. When the person holding the item is finished, they pass the item to the person to their left so that person may speak. The item will go from person to person giving each individual a voice in the circle. The item may travel around the circle several times to allow for further input from each individual.

This form of medicine, the talking circle, is one of the principal tools to carry the teachings of our brothers and sisters. It is a way to inform others of the teachings of the people and to allow each individual to heal within the circle.

The healing that comes from circles is strong and varied. It might be a healing between people or an individual healing of various people in the circle. Hearing others often lends healing to each other in their own circumstances. The healing may show itself in various ways emotionally, physically, spiritually and/or mentally. Often times we do not even realize the healing is occurring or we do not feel the impact of it until long after. This is a natural way of caring for one another as helpers. We are all ska be Wis, helpers.

Nish Nung and I would often call for circles and invite those who had expressed an interest to attend. As we would call for these circles the people would come. Generally there would only be a few. Circles as small as four or five and usually not bigger than fifteen people. It seems like far more people are interested in going to powwows than going to a place for ceremony and healing. Sometimes people would come looking for help with illnesses. Nish Nung would not refuse anyone and was always ready to help. "It does not matter who the person is", he would say. "They are our relatives and we should help anyone that asks. We must never judge anyone or refuse anyone. It is one thing to look at ones actions and another to look at the person. You should not judge someone when you have not traveled in their shoes."

My work in the circles started by being there and participating when the feather would move to me. The circles began for me when I met you, Misho, and watched the way you would do them. I was learning from those who have been attending over the years and sharing from my experiences the best I could.

As Nish Nung and I would do circles, he would ask me to ska be wis [be a helper]. I would prepare the circle area and the people for the circle. In these circles ceremony was always used to open and close the circle. The leaders of the circle would share at'izookan, stories of the people, with a teaching and then allow the feather to travel around the circle. My work was to help the people and Spirit in this way. As the circles continued, I realized that the teachings gifted to me and the teachings I share with others are the way to help the people.

When Nish Nung was not able, I would lead the circle. I began to call for circles or go to where they were asked for throughout New England. Sometimes there would be ten to fifteen people. Other times there might only be one. I would get upset at traveling hundreds of miles and find that only one or two people would come. As I would process my discontent, I could hear Spirit respond. "Do the circle! It doesn't matter whether others come or not. Just do it and in time they will come."

This, seemingly, exercise in futility of holding ceremony when so many would ask and so few would come, has been a great lesson for me in my life. If you want something to happen, you have to show up.

Recently my son Nick and I traveled into Canada from New Hampshire to support the Ojibwe Grandmother Water Walkers. They were walking the last part of a five year walk around the great Lakes and to the ocean to honor the water. The walk was vision of an Ojibwe Grandmother to bring attention to the need to protect and respect the water and its' life giving properties.

We pulled out from Amherst, New Hampshire at three in the morning to try to arrive along the St. Lawrence River at the point where they would be walking by ten o'clock. Our hope was that several others would come with us, but as the others came to realize the distance and barriers that would have to be crossed, we saw our group dwindle down to the two of us. This was a little disappointing, since it meant that we had no women to help with the carrying of the water. Nevertheless, we made the best of it and when we arrived we did what we could to help.

We found two Grandmothers carrying the water. They would take turns walking about a quarter mile each and then passing the copper water pail to each other. There were two men who also would take turns accompanying them with a feather staff, signifying the ceremony of the walk. We spent the day helping where we could as they walked into a Mohawk reservation along the St. Lawrence River. It was a beautiful experience for both Nick and me to be helpers in this ceremony.

That evening we began our drive back to New Hampshire from some place near Montreal, Canada. Nick commented that it seemed hardly worthwhile to go to all that trouble when so few seemed to be helping. I explained to him that others would be there and are coming, and some people who had been there had to go back home for various reasons. He replied that he felt hundreds or more should have been walking. His comments made both of us realize how very important it is to support the good works of our brothers and sisters. It was a good day and we arrived safely home from our journey, only wishing that we could have stayed longer.

"I hear you spirit! I just need to show up!"

It was now late in the afternoon and Misho decided to stay one more night. Noodin and Misho went down to town for dinner. As they entered a restaurant in Jaffrey, New Hampshire they could not help but notice that everyone stopped what they were doing and looked at them. There are not many native people around New Hampshire and the ones who are don't look so Indian as to be noticeable. Misho was dressed pretty much like everyone else, but wore a hat that had an Eagle and the words "Native Pride" written across the side. A small pin was on the hat that said "hug the Shaman".

They sat down and a waitress took their order. Sitting across from them was a local police officer. The officer would not stop looking at the two of them. Misho and Noodin paid no attention to him and ate their dinner. As they got up to leave, Noodin looked at the officer and politely said "good evening". The police officer just stared as they left and no further comment was made about this incident. It is sad to know that there are so many places where anyone who is different is suspiciously scrutinized.

In years past, I would not have had any idea of how Misho might have felt in that situation. Having been on many reservations over the years, I have experienced the same thing from my red brothers who did not know me when I have visited places there. It is a sad thing when others react in a way that makes one feel unwelcome.

CHAPTER TWELVE

The Medicines

~ **Migizii** ~ [bald eagle] Bald Eagle that carries the prayers of the people to Gizhi Manidou, Great Spirit, to demonstrate the love of the people for Creator.

Noodin and Misho got up at sunrise and had a morning ceremony to greet the day. Misho was sitting by the fire in Noodin's camp at Monadnock State Park relaxing. He would be leaving the next morning for Lake Lena in Minnesota to go home. They would spend the day traveling around to visit Sussy, John and Rona and Zhinqwak.

That evening they returned to Noodin's cabin and sat in his camp by the fire.

"You know, Noodin," Misho commented, "traveling with Nish Nung must have taught you a lot about medicines we use for the people. It is all medicine you know. Everything that we do in this walk is about healing and being all that we can be in a good way.

What do you feel that the medicines have done for you? All that you have told me that has happened to you is about healing and helping others to heal. How do you understand medicines now?"

Noodin looked up from the fire. The sky was filled with stars and the smoke from the fire was swirling gently toward them. Sometimes the smoke would block a star or two and then disappear and the star would be back in its place. It was almost as if the smoke were making the stars blink.

The forest was quiet and peaceful. No other people were camping that night so the whole seven thousand acres was occupied by only two men. Noodin and Misho sat quietly sharing an understanding that was a way of life of this man, Misho. Noodin felt as if he were gifting back in some way to Misho and Misho's ancestors by coming to know these ways. Noodin was comfortable now with Misho and felt as if he were like a grandfather to Noodin, though Misho was only fifteen or more years older than Noodin.

Noodin answered; "I don't know much, Misho. The more that you and others show me the more I realize how little I actually do know. In many ways that is a gift. I do not have to feel like I have all, or for that matter any, of the answers. The burdens of holding many things have been taken away. I have come to realize that most of the things that I thought were so very important like property, more clothes than I need, money, new cars, a business, a house, being recognized in the community and all these material things are really just ego filling because of what I have been conditioned to think. Our modern world seems to be bent on convincing the people that they have to be driven toward success and feeding the economy in order to be happy. It is ironic to me that in my experience it is just the reverse. I find happiness today in seeking to know and share what I learn with others who wish to find answers as well. Many like me begin to seek, without really understanding what or why they are seeking.

There are no new beginnings. When we know, then we understand that we know little. When we move we are only traveling in the next of a series of circles some call the natural order. To be where you are is only because you have come to that place from another place. The present is the reality we seek though we often look in every place but the present. To be one with self is the goal and the reward is to be at one with all that is."

"Yes!" Misho replied. "You are beginning to see. The healing is in coming to know the dibwewin (di bway win, truth]. To be centered is to seek an understanding of all that you are within yourself and all that is around you. As you become aware of the dibwewin, the centering stabilizes and you find balance in your life."

"So Misho, the medicine is what we come to understand that keeps us balanced in our daily lives. Is that right?" Noodin asked.

"I don't know." Misho answered. "That is what I believe to be part of it and that makes it real for me. It is up to you to find the answers you believe."

Noodin replied; "If medicine is all things, most people miss it because they tend to buy into the Western concept of medicine. We tend to think medicine is something only applicable if it has to do with a doctor, pharmaceutical or a hospital treatment."

Misho answered; "All that is that supports life is medicine Noodin."

"Yes! I see that. There are many definitions of medicine." Noodin answered.

These are the definitions of medicine that are recognized within modern society in this time:

Medicine Wikipedia, the free encyclopedia

Medicine is the art and science of healing. It encompasses a range of health care practices evolved to maintain and restore health by the prevention and treatment of illness.

The American Heritage® Dictionary - (5 definitions)

(mĕdĭ-sĭn) [Middle English, from Old French, from Latin medicīna, from feminine of medicīnus, of a doctor, from medicus, physician; see medical.]

(noun)

Modern Dictionary

The science of diagnosing, treating, or preventing disease and other damage to the body or mind.

1. *The branch of this science encompassing treatment by drugs, diet, exercise, and other nonsurgical means.*

2. *The practice of medicine.*

3. *An agent, such as a drug, used to treat disease or injury.*

4. *Something that serves as a remedy or corrective: medicine for rebuilding the economy; measures that were harsh medicine.*

5. *Aboriginal*

6. *Shamanistic practices or beliefs, especially among Native Americans.*

7. *Something, such as a ritual practice or sacred object, believed to control natural or supernatural powers or serve as a preventive or remedy.*

"The question remains, Noodin," Misho said "what have the medicines done to help you heal?"

Noodin answered; "The medicines of the people are profound in many ways.

It begins with Spirit. There are four medicines that are the most important in the teachings. They are called the four chiefs. They are: asema [a say ma – tobacco], wiinagush [wee na goosh – sweet grass], mushkadebug [moosh ka day bug – sage] and giizhikandug [gee zhi ka dug – white cedar].

The asema – tobacco is the medicine of the eastern direction. It is used to offer prayer for everything and is very powerful in transcending prayer to spirit world and the creator.

The wiinagush – sweet grass is the medicine of the south direction and offers protection in spirit world for the family.

The mushkadebug – sage is the medicine of the western direction and offers protection in spirit world for the community.

Giizhikandug – white cedar is the medicine of the northern direction and offers cleansing of the people and all that is around the people.

These are the first medicines to be used in a ceremony and they may be used continually as the ceremony progresses in healing of the people. These medicines basically open the door to spirit world for healing and communication. There are many teachings and legends for these medicines in order to utilize them in a good way."

"Yes!" Misho answered. "Many teachings, many stories."

Noodin continued; "The medicines sit in certain directions. The directions I have been given are as the Ojibwe people apply them and they may vary by tribe and teachings but they do the same things for the people.

The four directions where these medicines are placed are the four compass directions. They are part of seven directions that include additionally the sky, the earth and below.

Spirit preparation is essential to any healing of the people in medicine healings of the people.

All healing starts with Spirit. It begins with smudging utilizing sage, and an offering of tobacco to honor Spirit. If done in the traditional way, they will honor all of the medicines of all the directions including sky, earth and below."

Misho stood and went to put some wood on the fire. The evening was becoming cool and the fire needed to be well fed.

Noodin went into his cabin and brought out a blanket for his teacher to help him stay warm. He then freshened Misho's coffee. "I find it difficult, Misho, to find any definition that really describes the medicines of the people as you have shown me. In the world we live in today, it brings to mind what is said of the ancient Celtic traditions. What they carried in Spirit has been lost for so long that no one can remember. It seems like that is how it is with the medicines

I have heard many speak of the medicines and what they are, how they work and even how to work with them. I do not believe any medicine is good or bad. It is how the medicine is used that makes it choose to be one or the other. If one takes two aspirin they can clear a headache. If one consumes a bottle of aspirin they can die. It is the same with all medicine."

Misho answered; "That is true, Noodin, and recognizing that means it is the knowledge and application of the medicines that tell what they will do."

Noodin said; "Even the air and water we take in to maintain life is a medicine. Without it we would quickly expire and a lack of it can make us become ill. Too much of it will kill us and we need to receive it in a proper amount to maintain our health. This is also true of all of our brothers and sisters regarding the medicine of air and water. Only the right amounts will continue the health of life for ourselves and all of our brothers and sisters.

All medicines affect life on a multiple basis. We are affected emotionally, physically, spiritually and mentally. If the medicine is applied in a way of honoring these four parts of who we are we can maintain a place of wellness. If we treat only a part of who we are then there is the continuation of the illness, either as it is or in some other way. Understanding medicine in this way creates a different approach that is ancient in teachings to help one another.

All life has the ability to heal. Recent scientific research has concluded that when something enters a forest that can be harmful to that forest, a healing process begins. A communication between the plants somehow occurs. An invading worm might enter a tree and begin to cause injury or disease to the tree. That tree alerts all of the surrounding forest that it is under attack. The other life in the forest immediately starts to create, or attempt to create, a deterrent to push away the invader. It is interesting that science discovers these things that have been known by aboriginal healers for thousands, if not more, years."

"I don't know much about science, Noodin." Misho answered. "It seems that sometimes the scientists and doctors are so busy trying to figure out the truth that they look past what has already been given to us by Spirit through our ancestors. They think they have all the answers and they don't even know the question."

"I guess," Noodin replied, "to me it comes down to just what does it mean to heal and how do I do it for myself and others around me? First, I need to understand communications. We tend to think that we are only talking when we speak from our mouth, hear when we listen with our ears, see when we look with our eyes, taste when we taste with our tongue, smell when we smell with our nose and feel when we touch. This is how it may seem, but I find that there is more to it.

When I speak, I speak with feeling in my body, my eyes, my mouth, my hearing, my sense of taste, my sense of smell and a sense of how I am being heard. All of my senses work at the same time and all are involved. It is the same when I hear, touch, see, smell, taste and sense. As I have become aware of this in myself it has made me more aware of myself and of everything around me. Sometimes when I put this in words, Misho, it sounds kind of corny but it is real to me and I do not question it. The awareness that this realization brings opens up whole new avenues of understanding and communication. It all ties into the medicines and how they affect others as well as myself."

"You are beginning to understand, Noodin."

Noodin continued; "As it pertains to the medicines, it tells me that a simple aspirin to cure a headache may not be the answer. First I have to have the truth of the illness. The truth being a full understanding of everything about the headache. Its' true cause. Where did it come from, what else may be happening, where I am and what I am doing to name a few. To cure the head ache I can take an aspirin but to cure the illness I may have to take a more holistic approach. I need to look at what is going on physically, mentally, emotionally and spiritually. I can take the aspirin for the headache and bodily pains but I also need to ask Spirit for guidance and help. I need to take steps to seek balance. Balance begins with the understanding I am out of balance and determining where I am out of balance. I may be affected because my friend had an argument with me and I feel hurt, emotionally. As I think about it I become wound up in the emotion mentally and project more negativity toward the illness. As I have become emotional and mental over it I pay little or no attention to the physical effect and the spiritual effect. I am then out of balance. I am somewhere in my four directional thinking between mental and emotional. To be centered, I try to be in the center of the emotional, physical, spiritual and mental parts of who I am. When I realize this I can take the aspirin to relieve the headache and maybe take a walk and ask for Spirit to focus with me to change the concentration from the mental and tenseness of the emotion that is going on. If I do this in earnest I am healing the cause and finding the balance I need to be well. Not always as easy to do as it is to say but the more one tries the easier it gets.

The same approach seems to be what the medicine people assist us in doing. Earlier I told you Misho about Nish Nung doctoring Wabigwan It is always amazing to see these things done to help the people. In looking at what is done one can see the process of healing that takes place.

The healer, medicine man, first determines what the possible causes are for the sickness.

Nish Nung started asking her questions. She responded with information pertaining to her illnesses and also experiences in her life walk that might reflect reasons for the illnesses that were inflicted.

The healer and his helper then start to prepare the area for a healing ceremony, asking Spirit to help in the healing.

I smudged the room and all of us. This would set up a protection boundary and invite Spirit to come to help in the ceremony. Then Nish Nung took out his pipe and lit it. He offered prayers in his language for Rebecca and all people who suffer from sickness.

As the ceremony began the Spirit was alerted to come in to help.

Nish Nung told me to take my drum and to begin drumming. Don't stop drumming until I am finished, he said.

I began to drum as Nish Nung took out medicine stones and gave them to Rebecca with instruction to hold them as he continued.

Utilizing the energy of spirit through the medicine man and the feather, the healer begins a process to locate the illness and begin to remove it.

He took a bald eagle feather and began to pass the feather over her as if he were searching for something. He would chant as he did this, and now and then he would stop in certain places and concentrate on particular areas of her body.

When he finished, I stopped the drum. We sat there while Rebecca got back into her wheel chair.

The person with the illness is praying and seeking strength through Spirit to heal.

She seemed calmer than before and moved a little easier.

Medicines are brought out and applied that are known to help physically. They are first prepared and Spirit is directed to seek the specific illnesses being treated.

Nish Nung reached into his bag and took out a root that he was carrying with him. He gave it to me and instructed me to grind it into a fine grain.

He boiled a cup of water, and took a pinch of the root and put it into the water. He handed it to Rebecca. Drink this, he said. Drink a cup of this everyday and it will work to make you well.

Nish Nung then reached in his bag and took out a bottle that contained a salve. He asked Rebecca for a silver spoon and used it to take a spoonful of the salve from the bottle. He put it in a small glass for her. Nish Nung then said, "Put this on your hands every day. It will last a long time and it doesn't take much. It will relieve the pain in your hands and give you use of them again."

The medicines used to heal in this case: Communication to prepare mentally and make aware as well as to help calm the emotion. Sage to prepare the area, the pipe to offer prayer, stones to gather the sickness and offer Spirit energy, a feather to identify and move and heal in the ceremony, a drum to call Spirit, singing to energize the prayer requests to Spirit by the medicine man, his helper, others and the person, a root known to help certain illnesses identified made into a tea, a salve to treat an illness of the bones and within the body.

The medicine man also, with the training, gifts of spirit and energy of prayer is able to extract the illness and take it within himself. He will often become sick from this and will carry it for a time to release it in a place where it will do no harm to others. This is the part that I asked Nish Nung about when he answered; "I do not really know. I can only tell you that as I use the feather or other tools and pray, I feel a sense of direction from Spirit that tells me what is wrong and guides me as to what to do. I trust in the guidance of spirit. As for the medicines I use, they are passed down from Elders who carry that knowledge. "

Misho responded; "All that you have seen and much more, Noodin. We all have ways to help others heal. That does not make us medicine men. The gifts of Spirit together with a lifetime of teachings from Elders are needed to give the medicine man all that he needs to do that work. Remember the legend, Noodin. Remember that Spirit put the medicines out throughout the land and certain of the people began to gather the medicines. Those were the people of the Midewiwin and they were gifted the knowledge to use those medicines. Do not be fooled by just anyone who claims to be a medicine man."

"One more thing, Misho." Noodin commented. "Today I know who I am, I know where I came from and I know where I am going."

"Then the medicine is working, Noodin." Misho answered.

"We should get some rest, Misho. You have a long trip in the morning."

"Mino dibit Noodin. [Good night Wind]" Misho said as he entered the cabin to rest.

CHAPTER THIRTEEN

Carry the Message

~ *Nbaa kaa win* ~ [**wisdom**] Use the wisdom for the people. The understanding that is gained through interacting with all things that are of the creation.

There is never a bad time to travel through Wisconsin. One of the most beautiful times is in the early autumn when farmers are harvesting their crops and the fields are a lush green. Traveling over the rolling hills and seeing new verandas of beauty each time one peaks a hill.

Usually Noodin travels west through Canada and the scenery is very different but equally as beautiful. This time he wanted to visit with Misho before going to ceremony in northern Wisconsin. Traveling the southern route to Lake Lena, Minnesota is about the same distance as the northern route and Noodin decided to take the Wisconsin route for a change in scenery.

As Noodin pulled in the driveway at Misho's home he could see Misho sitting on the porch smoking a cigarette while whittling something from a stick.

Noodin got out of the car and went up on the porch. He sat in a chair next to Misho and lit a cigarette. Neither said anything right away. The long drive had taken most of the talk out of Noodin and Misho was busy notching away at the wood carving in his lap.

Misho spoke first; "Booshoo, Noodin, annii aezha aa yaa yaan," [greetings wind, how are you?]

"Nimii noo aa yaa, giindash." [I am fine, and you.]

"Nimii noo aa yaa. Mino giizhigut." [I am fine. It is a good day.]

"Eh." [yes.]

Misho, "What have you been up to Noodin?"

"I have been traveling a lot, Misho. I've been visiting with people of all ages, especially young adults around the country."

Misho, "Are you still doing work with those youth places in Pennsylvania?"

"Yes, I am still doing work with VisionQuest in Pennsylvania and in Florida too. It is a good feeling when you connect with a kid, Misho."

Misho asked; "how did you get hooked up with those people, Noodin? The VisonQuest people."

"There was a ceremony near my place in Amherst, New Hampshire when I lived there. A Micmac Elder, Grandfather Albert, was coming down from Canada to do a ceremony for about fifty people. His fire keeper couldn't make it so a woman called me and asked if I could help. The woman had heard that I had put together talking circles around New England and that I had teachings as a fire keeper. She needed fire wood, saplings for the lodge and grandfathers [stones] for the lodge. I agreed to gather the things they needed and help to build the lodge. When I got there, I helped put everything together and agreed to be their fire keeper.

As people began to arrive I would greet them and introduce myself. I was in the parking lot when a truck pulled in with New Brunswick, Canada license plates. Two men got out and walked over to me. The older of the two men asked me if I knew Watie Akins from Old Town, Maine. I told him that I knew Watie, and that he is a friend of mine. The man introduced himself as Irving and told me he was hoping to see Watie at the ceremony. I told him that I had talked to Watie and he told me he wasn't going to make it due to health problems.

Watie is a Penobscot Elder and I knew him from ceremonies in Wisconsin. He is getting on in years and doesn't travel much anymore.

Irving introduced me to the younger man, Ed Perley, aka Eedee aach / Blue Jay from the Tobic Reservation in New Brunswick, Canada. Ed is from the Maliseet First Nation people.

During breaks in the ceremony Irving, Ed and I spent as much time together as we could visiting and getting to know each other and share teachings. Irving's Medicine Wheel Teachings were much like yours and he was helpful to me in understanding the teachings. We spent all night talking about different aspects of the Medicine Wheel.

At a social that was held on the last night of the gathering, people were invited to sing songs and tell stories. Ed acted as the announcer for the event. He asked me if I would tell the legend of how the flute came to the people. I did the legend and it was well received by everyone.

When the ceremony ended Irving and Ed departed for New Brunswick, Canada and I went home. I did not hear from them again and thought nothing more about it other than the memory of experiencing teachings from Irving.

Several months passed and I was in Maine to do a Story Telling presentation at the University of Maine. I was camping up near Freeport, Maine on that trip. The night before I was to do the presentation I got a call from Ed Perley. He told me he was traveling down to Pennsylvania to do some work and wanted to know if I wanted to come to help. I told him that I had a commitment but would come after that and he replied that it was now or it could not happen. I declined due to my commitment to the University of Maine.

Ed told me he was asking because Irving had suggested that I could be helpful in the work that Ed does as a story teller.

The next day Ed called back. He informed me that he had to return to Tobic because an Elder had passed over. He asked if I could travel with him in two weeks and I told him that would work.

Ed would not tell me exactly where we were to go or exactly what we would be doing other than that we would be working with kids.

Two weeks passed and Ed pulled up to the house in Amherst, New Hampshire. I loaded in my pack, bundle case, drum and flute case, a jacket, sleeping bag and pillow. "We are ready to go", I announced.

"You can drive. I need a break", Ed replied.

His truck was a 2004 F-150 with an extended cab. Nice vehicle and it road very well for a truck.

It was an eight hour drive from Amherst, New Hampshire down to southern Pennsylvania and we stopped once to top our gas. I drove the distance and Ed talked most of the way. His talking kept me awake and that was a good thing.

We pulled into an area someplace near Gettysburg and checked into a hotel around three in the morning. It was good to finally reach a place to rest and we slept in until ten. We went to breakfast and then started to our destination. It was a winding road up a mountain to a place called South Mountain Camp.

I still did not really know where I was, who we were to work for, or what the whole deal was all about. Just that we would do sweat lodges and ceremony for some inner city kids. Ed told me the company we would be working for was VisionQuest.

When we arrived at the facility Ed went inside to talk to the director. I waited in the car. I called Monica, my ex-wife and told her, "I am someplace in southern Pennsylvania at a place called VisionQuest. That is all I know at this point." I was just letting her know where I was to pass that on to the kids.

A few minutes later she called me back. "Jim, do you remember what you were trying to put together when we met." I answered; "Yeah, an after treatment place for kids. A six month program that would be on a ranch in Durango with horses paired up with the kids and ongoing value structuring programs." "Yes", she said. "Well, that was twenty years ago and you just went full circle. That is what VisionQuest does, only as an alternative correctional facility for juveniles." I was quiet for a moment as I realized the weight of what she was saying to me. Tears were in my eyes as I acknowledged that what she had said was true. Yet Another affirmation of the teachings. All things travel in a circle.

Ed and I went into the office to meet the staff. They all knew Ed and he kept introducing me as an Elder that he brought with him. I pulled Ed aside. "Ed, I am not an Elder, I am just a helper." Ed answered; "To me you are an Elder. You know a lot and have it to share. You know more about a lot of native teachings than I do and I grew up an Indian. Irvin regards you as a fellow Elder and I know other Elders that do too." I answered; "You shouldn't tell people I am an Elder. I don't think of myself that way and my Elders would not appreciate that people might refer to me as an Elder. I have to be careful with the things that have been gifted to me, Ed."

Ed continued to introduce me to the various people leaving the Elder thing out. "This is Gerry Fox, He is the director of this facility and this is Jerry Barios, director of the native fabric program."

We had a meeting and determined that we would stay at South Mountain for ten days. Then we would stop at two other facilities in the middle of the state and then go up to Big Lodge in Franklin, Pennsylvania for the last five days of work. Ed took me for a walk around the camp and explained a little about VisionQuest and the work they do.

VisionQuest is a national organization dedicated to providing an alternative to juvenile detention centers throughout the United States. The program is similar to other programs also provided around the country. The difference is that VisionQuest utilizes Native American teachings to introduce positive values to the youth kept at the facility. The teachings that they use were given to VisionQuest by an Elder of the Crow people out west. In the East they have been utilizing tribal Elders from the eastern tribes. The values are similar amongst the tribes, so different Elders easily can be incorporated to assist in the program. That is what we were there for, to assist in the program.

In the middle of the camp was a large Teepee with a ring of stones next to it. To the side was a sweat lodge with a fire pit in front of it. I looked inside the sweat lodge and noticed that the womb of mother earth, the hole dug in the lodge was located at the side near the east door of the lodge. Lodges that I had used always had the hole dug in the center of the lodge. Ed explained that this was a buffalo lodge and that the hole was dug where the heart of the buffalo would be. The buffalo lodge has different teachings but basically the same concept. As we walked around the camp, some of the kids would wave to Ed and say hello. Ed would come here about once every two months. It was obvious that some of these kids had been here for some time and liked when Ed and others would come to work with them. There was a fully equipped school for the kids with a full teaching staff including a principal, a mess hall, and several barracks to house the kids, a medical building, administrative building and trailers where some of the staff live full time. All of this in a beautiful setting in the Appalachian mountain range on South Mountain in Pennsylvania, not fifty feet off of the Appalachian Trail.

All of the personnel are given rank from corporal on up as in military type operations and each carried a two way radio to stay in contact. There are no fences around the perimeter and the kids are kept at close monitoring at all times. Both boys and girls are at this facility and all precautions are taken to assure that the boys and girls never come in contact with each other. The boys use parts of the facility when the girls are utilizing other parts of the facility.

Ed and I went over to the lodge and began to collect wood to start a fire to heat stones for the first sweat lodge. I laid back a little and watched Ed for the lead in putting everything together. He kind of was doing the same thing and waiting to see how I would do it. Since he had been there before and had a system, I wanted to be respectful of the way he was used to doing things. He, on the other hand, wanted to see if I did it differently. The work got done and pretty soon a group of young men came down to the fire.

"Ears!" Ed said. "Open!" The young men replied. Ed began to introduce them to me and prepare for the lodge. On this first lodge, Ed and I would both go in and he would be the conductor. Since I had not conducted a lodge it is important that he work with me to be sure that I know what to do and how to do it. We entered the lodge and Ed told me to conduct the lodge. When the lodge was done and we were putting things away Ed told me; "You conduct lodge as well as anyone I have been in a sweat with." I explained that with his guidance, I will conduct lodges at VisionQuest. He agreed. We heated up more rocks and Ed went in and conducted a sweat lodge for another group of boys.

When we finished doing sweat lodges it was about nine thirty at night and we were hungry. Barios invited us to join him to find a place to eat. He took us into a town nearby and to a bar by some railroad tracks in a lower part of the town. We went into RobRoys Bar and Grill. It was a dance bar that had food served until closing. By the time we got there it was eleven thirty and the place was really hopping. When we entered there was a bouncer at the door and he frisked each of us as we came in. Barios seemed to know a lot of people there and began talking to various people at the bar. Ed found a seat at the bar and I found one down the bar a way and next to Barios. The man next to Ed was a black man who was really intoxicated. That man decided that Ed must be a cop and told him he should move to a different seat. Ed suggested that if that man did not like him, since he wasn't bothering anybody, that that man move. Fortunately, Barios knew the guy and quickly put the altercation to rest. As soon as a seat opened up, Ed moved down with us and we enjoyed the best chicken wings and macaroni that I had ever had. The bar brought back a lot of memories of the days that I would go bar hopping when I was younger. It was, strangely, a somewhat nostalgic feeling, though I am glad that I don't have to do that anymore. Barios had four or five beers while we were there while Ed and I ate and waited to get out of there. It was strange to me that Barios was drinking because he explained to me earlier that he was a Sun Dancer and drinking is taboo in that following. Well it is not for me to judge but it did make an impression and had an effect on how I accept the things he does and says. Maybe I am being a little judgmental. When someone claims to be one thing and then does something else that is contrary it is prudent in my mind to be careful.

The next morning we went over to the lodge and started a fire around ten thirty. We kept the fire going until about two o'clock before the first kids came over for ceremony. It seemed to me a long time to have to keep a fire heated to keep the stones red hot. Apparently the scheduling for this part of their program was somewhat on a when convenient level to the people. I asked Ed if this was the norm and he assured me that it was. That and heating enough rocks all at once for several sweat lodges to be run consecutively meant a huge amount of firewood and continuous care of the fire. It was only my place to be there for those kids but it did appear that a better system could have been put in place. At least they had a good supply of wood and I would later find that having the wood on hand was a blessing. We did two lodges that day. When we finished the last lodge, a man in a light brown suit and sporting a handle bar mustache came up to us and said hello. Ed knew him and introduced me to him. Jim, this is Tom Laser, Superintendant of the school here for the kids.

Tom stated; "I understand that you are a story teller, Noodin."

"Well I have done storytelling and I do a program in the state park system up in New Hampshire."

Tom said; "I wonder if you would be willing to do story telling in our classes tomorrow for both the boys in the morning and the girls in the afternoon."

"Sure" I replied, "I would be happy to do that."

"Fine" Tom said, Come over to the school at eight thirty tomorrow and we will get you started."

In the morning I gathered my flute case and drum bag. Ed and I went up to the school and entered the first class. There where ten young men together with a guard in the class. None of the boys seemed very responsive and the attitude in the class vibrated with tenseness. The teacher had everyone sit down and introduced Ed and myself.

Ed began, "I am Ed and I am a Maliseet Indian from up north in Canada. Before we start I want all of you to know the rules. There aren't any, other than no speaking. You can listen, draw, read or sleep while Jim tells you the legend. Before I bring Noodin up I want each of you to take a big breath and hold it. Now let it out. Take another. Now let it out. Take another. Now let it out. This helps us to all focus on the same thing. Noodin is an Elder and a story teller so I will let him tell you about himself."

I kind of smirked at Ed for bringing up the Elder thing again. I could not help but wonder how these kids would respond to the stories I would tell. After all, these kids, for the most part, were inner city kids from Philadelphia and Pittsburg. They were here for committing anything from school absenteeism to drug peddling and gang related violence. Now I am going to tell them stories and these guys are really going to listen? It almost sounded like wishful thinking in my mind. I noticed one young black man that never looked up and just kept drawing with a pencil from the time he entered the room and sat down. No one messed with him and basically let him be.

I started. "Boo shoo, that means hello in Ojibwe. The Ojibwe are the largest nation of Indians in North America. The Navaho are the largest tribe in the United States but the Ojibwe live in the United States and Canada up around the Great Lakes. The elders teach that the legends begin with the beginning and that is where I will start."

I began to tell a story; "There was a time, long ago. Gichie Manidou, great spirit, was all alone in the darkness - - -"

As I told the story, Ed watched the kids. When I am telling the story I kind of lose a sense of those around me. I may interact with one or another of the kids as I tell the story but I am not selective based on who is paying attention and who is not. The room became completely still as I went on. You could feel that everyone in the room was focused as we progressed, together, through the great time of creation. The young men, so hardened because of their circumstances, were transfixed in the story. At the end I went around and shook the hand of each person in the room and thanked them for allowing me to share. After the young men left, the teacher told me that this was the most relaxed class he had ever experienced while working at VisionQuest. Something had happened. These kids were hungry for answers. Answers to questions they had no knowledge of.

Ed and I went to the next class. It was the same kind of thing. The teacher would introduce Ed and me and then Ed would start off with the breathing exercise. I would introduce myself and we would start.

"After the great flood, the people were few and they were weak. So weak that sometimes just walking through the forest, they would trip over a root of a tree and fall down and die - - -."

Again, the young men in the room were completely transfixed. At the end of the story I told them about my walking stick and asked Ed to sing a Maliseet song with the drum. Ed is a beautiful singer and his songs in his language have a beautiful sound. Again we shook hands with each person there and thanked them for allowing us to share.

When the third group of young men came in, they were all excited. Hey man! You're going to tell us stories. We hear you are pretty good man! Lets' get it on. They were psyched and a little over the top. I thought to myself, now we get it. We will never calm these kids down.

Same routine, Ed did the breathing exercise and I began the story.

"Weno Booshoo asked Nochomis one day, what happened to my father, Nochomis? Hooo, she replied, he has gone on to Spirit world and watches us from the west. Yes, but what happened to make him leave, Weno Booshoo persisted. He did battle with a great spirit that kills everything with disease, Nokomis answered, and that spirit killed him. Who is this - - -."

Again the young men were silent and totally into the story. We finished again with Ed's drum song. The teacher couldn't believe it. I have never seen this class sit so quietly. They all got into it. As they left we greeted each one of the young men and thanked them for allowing us to share. Many of them came up to us before we could get to them.

That ended the morning and in the afternoon we would begin the same program with the young women. Ed commented to me. You know, you might think that these young men are hard to deal with but, believe me, the girls are even harder.

We were in the class room as the first group of about eight girls came in. Some were on meds and fairly calm. Others were easily excitable and you could hardly know what to expect. These were tough young girls with distressful histories. The teacher could barely get their attention to introduce us. Only a few of them followed Ed in the breathing exercises. I began.

"Booshoo, greetings in Ojibwe. The Ojibwe are my teachers."

Some of the girls would talk back at me after each thing I would say.

"So what?" One would say. "We don't care!" Another would respond.

"OK," I said. "There is only one rule. You can do anything while I talk but you have to allow me to finish the story before you speak. Can we do that?" I asked. "Yeah!" One answered.

I began to tell the story; "There was a time when there was much sickness. A great chief was concerned that so many of the people were sick and dying. He decided he needed to do something and went into a lodge to offer his acknowledgement to the spirits and ask for help. That night as he slept, his daughter died of the sickness. Gawiin! Which means No, he yelled. It is not her time! He called on three other chiefs to meet with him in council and he told them that he had heard that there is a way to bring his daughter back, because it was not her time. One of the chiefs replied that he had heard that there was a way - - -."

Again, there was total silence in the room as I told the story. These young women were as hungry for these things as the boys were in the morning.

"- and she looked at her father and said; I have brought with me the healing dance for the people and she began to dance around the fire. The jingle dress rang in rhythm with the dance and the men picked up their drums and began to beat to the speed of her dance. People began to come out of their lodges to see - - -"

I finished the story. Ed played the drum as I told parts of the story and I would dance as if I were the girl in the story. The girls would laugh a little at my imitation of a young Indian maiden dancing but it was happy laughter and that was good.

At the end, Ed and I went around and thanked each of the girls. They were smiling and calm. Thank you, said one of the more outspoken young ladies. I feel better.

I almost began to cry to see how these young, so called, hardened girls, were affected.

At the end of the day I looked at Ed and said. "This is a great day! I feel like we actually reached those kids." Ed replied, "You didn't tell the same story over again even once all day. How many stories do you know anyway?" I answered; "I don't know how many. I never counted. I listen at the fire when my Elders tell the teachings and I tell the stories the way I hear them. It is amazing to me how easily I can recall what they tell me. Some of these stories are written down in different places but I only tell those that I have heard told to me. I think they express more when they come from the heart."

Ed answered; "They sure did today. One of the sergeants in the second bungalow has asked if we would stop by there before taps and tell a story to the kids. Are you up to it?"

"Sure," I answered. "I will tell them how the flute came to the people and we can finish it with flute and drum songs."

"Sounds good" said Ed. "I will let him know we will be there."

We went out for dinner and came back at about eight o'clock. The staff was putting the boys through their routine of evening formation and then cleaning the area and showers when we got there. The boys then had to form up in front of their beds and then the instructor told them to lie down at attention. He began; now we are going to listen to a story teller. You will pay complete attention. You will not talk. You will not move around. You will not read or draw. You will not do anything but listen.

At that point Ed went up to the instructor and talked to him for a minute. The instructor turned around and came back in. "Okay, forget everything I just said. Just relax and do what Ed says to do."

Ed began with the breathing exercise and then introduced me.

"It was long ago on the great prairies of the west in a small Sioux Indian village. There was a young boy there, about your age. He was not as big as his brothers. He wasn't so good looking either. The boy kind of felt like he didn't fit in that place, that village where - - -"

I had them. They were totally into the story. As I came to the boy trying to make the stick sing like the wind had. I handed my flute to one of the boys and told him to play it. He blew on it and no sound came out and he looked at me questioningly. After all, I had just played it before handing it to him. "That can't be right", I said. I handed it to another boy. He couldn't make a sound either. Then I went on; "the boy wondered why won't it play? - - -."

The kids were captivated by the story, taking in every little point in the story as if it was a morsel of candy to be savored.

I finished the story and played a song. Then Ed played a song with his drum. After that we let those who were awake try the drum and the flute. Five of those kids fell asleep during the story and we knew that was a good thing. These boys no longer seemed like young hoodlums. They were laughing and sharing and being kids. We were seeing who they really are in their hearts. Perhaps with some of them, we were the first to see that. What a gift!

As we left the instructor came outside. "You know", he said, if you guys want to come by tomorrow night we would love it. As a matter of fact you can come by every night. We have never had these kids go down so well and now they are completely quiet."

"Thank you", Ed and I both replied. "We will come by when we can."

That was the beginning of three years traveling with my brother Ed to work in Juvenile Corrections. The experience has been wonderful and I continue to be in touch with some of the kids that went through those programs.

In today's world I guess I feel that the focus has changed and now most people are more focused on the money. It is a shame really. Corporate interest and self interest seems to be more important to people today than helping one another.

In drug and alcohol recovery I learned that my personal experience, strengths and hopes are helpful to others trying to recover. Things that I did not consider of much interest to others seem to help others identify and break down their own denial system so that they can begin to change.

Misho, "Helping the people is important. It must have come to you from somewhere, Noodin. Where do you think you gained your interest in helping others from?"

"My parents I suppose. They were always helpful to others.

When I was very small I remember a man coming to the back door of the house. He was a hobo and had come up from the railroad about a half mile behind our home on the edge of town. He asked my mother if she could spare any food. I remember her going into the kitchen and making him some sandwiches and a glass of milk. While he sat on the back step eating, my mother went to the laundry room and gathered a pair of my dads' pants and a shirt and gave them to the man. That act of kindness has always stayed with me.

Both of my parents were active in the community. My dad was in Rotary and on the hospital board in the town I lived in. My mother would always help in charity groups in town and in the church.

Those things really count in making an impression on a young mind."

Misho, "You had good reinforcement Wind. You have a strong heart and with it a blood memory. It is good that you now listen to that memory. Together with your own experience you are growing."

CHAPTER FOURTEEN

We are all Connected

~ **Sabe** ~ [wild man] Wild man helped Weno Booshoo
to gain insight and wisdom.

So what? What is this red road thing? How much of red road do you
go? What's it worth?

Seeking an answer to what it is all about is a lifelong process.

As a child I only knew there must be some reason for being.
My motivation was to investigate and acquire knowledge to grow and
survive. It may not have seemed like that was what was happening at
the time, but naturally that is what we seek. I learned how to speak,
take care of my own basic needs, interact with others and look in
wonder at the environment around me.

Coming into being a juvenile, I was challenged to apply what
I had gained and accumulate more information for survival in a bigger
community. It was a time of trials to see what works and to test the
knowledge gained in living. A time to try new things and reach out to
be on my own.

Being an adult would test what had been gained through the time of new life and being a juvenile. It would be a time of taking responsibility for me and others. The making of a family and establishing a way to survive in the society of which I belonged. The experience gained over time would be tested and added to. The tests would wear on me and the things that I would use to take the pressure off would not work as well if at all. Most things at that time of life seemed of material importance and anything else would be peripheral. Anything of spirit was secondary to the seemingly prime directive to succeed and support a family. It is a time of life when one begins to wonder if all there is that exists is to survive and meet the expectations of loved ones, friends and society in general. Is there something more? That seems to become the driving question as one continues in life.

On a warm sunny summer day back in 1954, as I recall, I was about nine years old and was very bored that day. There was no one around to play with. Mom and dad were busy cleaning around the house and doing various projects that I wanted nothing to do with. I decided to take a walk and see if I could find Rex. Rex was a golden retriever that would periodically come around and hang out with my friends and me as we played. His name wasn't really Rex but we didn't know his real name so we called him Rex. I don't think he cared much because he would come to almost anything that we called him. He just seemed to know we were his friends and he liked being with us. His owner was a Nun and lived in a cottage at the edge of town. This place was about two miles away from my home and was owned by the Catholic Church. The Nuns ran a home there to care for people who were invalids. It was a big estate once owned by the Woodward family. They were the people who started the Jell-O Company, which is my home towns claim to fame. Maybe the people there were veterans from World War II or something. I really never did know for sure what they did there. It was a property where you just weren't supposed to go. The place was a big old estate, thirty or forty acres of land, and was surrounded by a large forested area. At the back of the estate was a small cottage where that Nun lived with her dog. I thought by walking down to the cottage maybe I would find Rex and play with him. Rex always liked to romp the fields when my friends and I were out exploring.

When I got near the estate I crossed a field and wandered up the dirt road along the back of the property, looking for Rex. I remember being very quiet so no one would discover that I was on the property.

Rex was nowhere to be found so I figured that he must be out wandering himself. I continued on my way up along a field near some bushes where my friend Philip and I had built a Fort. The bushes folded over like umbrellas making tunnels through the brush and we had cleared the spaces in the tunnels and made it into our little private Fort. I crawled in and started going to the different areas. I would sit in one place and then another just looking and listening. I remember it being very quiet so that any noise that was made was very distinct. If a bird moved on a branch you could hear it. I watched a Garter Snake quietly move across the ground near me and it looked so peaceful going along its way that I didn't even get scared. I never cared much for snakes. At one point I looked on the ground and saw a stick lying there that I did not remember having been there before. We had cleared the ground completely in our fort just a few days before and I wondered how that stick got there. I picked it up and looked at it. It was a very straight stick about five feet long. It was only about three-quarters of an inch thick but when I tried to break it, it would not break. First, I took hold of each end and tried to bend it. It would bend a little bit but it would not break. I was surprised at the strength of the stick. I held the stick at either end and put it to my knee and pulled back and still I could only bend it a little and it would not break. This was an unusual stick if I could not break it. I noticed that the stick had not been broken off from its original tree very long because the bark was still green. I left the little Fort of bushes after awhile and started to walk back home. I took the stick with me.

In the garage of my house I used a saw and cut the stick so that it was about four feet in length. That made a good length for a walking stick. I went out to the tree house in the back of my yard, climbed up, sat down and looked at my stick. This was my new walking stick. I took out my pocketknife and began to clean off some of the bark. First I peeled off the bark at the top of the stick so that it would have a clean handle to hold in my hand. Then I cleaned the bark off about 2 inches of the bottom of the stick so the bark would not look scruffy at the bottom. Then I found that because the bark was green, it peeled off easily when I cut into it. I began to cut designs into the bark. Sometimes I would cut crosses, sometimes a circle, serpentine like designs and diamond shapes. I cut designs all up and down that stick. When I was all done it looked really neat to me. I put the stick down in my room that night and it remained there for a month or so. When I looked at it again it'd dried and it still looked nice but not as fresh as when I had found it. I decided it needed something to protect it or the bark would eventually peel off and would not look so pretty. I took my new walking stick down to the garage and found some shellac my father had and painted that stick. Then I put the stick back in my room and went on with my life.

You know sometimes when you think back and remember some of the things you had as a child and you wonder what happened to them. What happened to my toy cars? Where did that blanket I liked go? I wonder where that stuffed bear went. What happened to the old lamp that was on my chest of drawers? Well for some reason that didn't happen with the walking stick. Over the years, wherever I went, I always took the stick with me. It wasn't that it was anything special, just that it was pretty and reminded me of that day in the little Fort in the bushes. Maybe the stick was a little special. For some reason that day, the day I found that stick, that was a special day. I did not know it then, but that day was a calm day in my life. It was a day when I was by myself on a really quiet gentle summer day with nature as my companion. Birds moving in the bushes, a snake crawling through the grass, a breeze rustling the leaves and an awareness of life all around me. My mind was quiet that day and my heart was listening.

In another time I sat at a fire after doing a ceremony the evening before going to court to process a divorce. As I sat there after closing the ceremony I could feel that calmness of being at one with all that is. It was a moment of being in the present. The ceremony had pulled me away from the memories of the past and the anxiety of the future and put me in the present.

Again, later that year, while coming out of fast, the feeling of the present once again was there. Only for an instant. Just when a breeze wrapped around me and held me in the love of creation. The past was gone for that moment and the future did not matter.

This walk has shown me a place where there is peace, tranquility and understanding. The present is the reality that we seek though we often look in every place but the present. To be one with self is the goal and the reward is to be at one with all that is. My red brothers and sisters have shown me many veils of life. The teachings that they so lovingly share have been freely given to change the story that is who I am.

It is not an easy thing to be in the present. Even a moment of being in the present is rare in my experience. The application of the stories, ceremonies, community, family and self discovery are what makes the connection. It is the connection to Spirit that allows one to release and live in the present. The trusting to Spirit gives one acceptance to focus and be at one with what is.

Being in the present is only a part of the answer. Understanding one's own reality and the reality of those around one is the other critical understanding. What one understands and the way that one understands it is what builds a belief system that guides a life. It does not have to be right or wrong. It is the experience and information that makes what one believes work or not for them. So what one believes is their personal understanding. It is their reality and it does not matter whether is true or not. It is what they know to be true.

Each of us believe things a little differently than another person. We define our truth based on the input and experience we gain over our time in life. What one believes as a youth may be completely different from what one believes as an adult but it is what that person knew to be true then. Since what we believe is the way it is for us, it often leads us to dispute what others may believe because they believe based on their own input. Their belief is the truth for them.

What Native teachings have shown me is that no two of us believe exactly the same thing and that we need to learn not to judge each other's reality or belief. It is the judging of the beliefs of one another that creates conflict and the conflict restricts the growth of the individual, family and community. Rather than judge one another it is important to respect each other's right to believe differently. When we respect others right to believe differently we are open to grow. We are not judging so much and can have dialogue and sharing. Through the dialogue and sharing often comes growth for all who are involved.

The first people of this land have another piece of their culture that cannot be ignored. It is the art of gifting. Native American gifting is a practice that goes back through the very thread of the culture. It is the cohesiveness of the people. When a gathering happens it is an accepted practice that the host will put out a blanket in the center of the gathering, called a giveaway, miigiwe, and put various items on the blanket. Each guest from eldest to the youngest will in turn go to the blanket and take one item of their liking. This will continue until there is nothing left on the blanket. Sometimes the blanket itself will also go as a part of the gifts offered. Some people have been known to give everything they have because they feel so honored by the people who visit them.

Ongoing gifting is a normal part of this practice. It is a custom to gift anyone that comes to visit. Often the host will gift something of significance to his guests. Always food will be offered as well, that no one will be hungry.

When something is done to help the people it is a gift of spirit. At a wedding the people come to witness the wedding. Gifting to the groom and the bride comes generally from within the family. The bride, groom and their families will have a giveaway at the end of the ceremony. The people attending will often gift to the newlyweds at some point during the following year to see that the needs of the new couple are meant. Gift the people that honor us rather than expecting gifts from them.

In our culture we use the term donation for giving. To the Native American that term means having pity on. Giving to the less fortunate. They do not see themselves as less than others.

Gifting is giving of yourself in return for a kindness that has been given to you. The kindness may be a material thing, a teaching, a healing or just a friendship and bonding between people. The importance of gifting is in the honoring of one another. It is not payment for something rather recognition of having respect of one another.

In this society it is difficult for indigenous people to offer the love of spirit through their teachings. In the past they would have been honored in return through the gifting of a blanket or trade item or something of need to them and of value. What was given was always acknowledged in some way.

Today our society says put a dollar amount on the item and we will pay you. This is contrary to the teachings of native culture.

In this writing each chapter has begun with a gift described and then the following chapter begins with description of an animal guide of that gift. These are given in the reverse order to the way they were told to me. The applications of these gifts have improved not just my life but the lives of many around me. The gifts are described below as they are given in the stories of the people of the Ojibwe. The people who I call my community. Those that I call my family.

The Seven Grandfather Teachings

Wisdom	~ *Nbaa kaa win* ~ Use the wisdom for the people. The understanding that is gained through interacting with all things that is of the creation.
Respect	~ *M'naa den d'mowin* ~ Respect everyone, all humans and all things created. Regard each with esteem and consideration. Allow others to believe in their reality.
Bravery	~ *Zoon gide'iwin* ~ Do things even in the most difficult times. Be ready to defend what you believe and what is right. Always stand up for the people.
Honesty	~ *Gwe kwaad ziwin* ~ Be honest in every action and provide good feelings in the heart. Do not be deceitful or use self-deception.
Humility	~ *Dbaad end'zin* ~ Know that you are equal to everyone else. Take pride in what you do, but the pride that you take is in the sharing of the accomplishment with others.
Love	~ *Zaa gidwin* ~ The love of life and creation that is felt by a seed planted as it senses the warmth of the soil heated by the sun. As it grows it pushes to the light and reaches out to feel the light and warmth. It honors the gift as it opens the petals of the flower to receive the bounties of life. It shares the bounties with all brothers and sisters that have need. Know this love and share it with all.
Truth	~ *Debwe win* ~ Understand all that is of those things that you use. Be true in everything that you do. Be true to yourself and true to your fellow man. Always speak the truth. Truth is the completeness and we only can know what we see.

The Seven Grandfathers

told the First Elder:

"Each of these teachings must be used with the rest; you cannot have wisdom without love, respect, bravery, honesty, humility and truth. To leave one out is to embrace the opposite of what that teaching is.

If one of these gifts is not used with the others, we will not be in balance. We must remember these teachings, practice them, and teach them to our children."

~ ~ ~ ~ ~ ~ ~ ~ ~ ~ ~ ~

As much as I have read and heard in my life that describes the feeling of spirit and creator, I have come to believe that it cannot be aptly described in words of any language.

The Spirit one feels in such a place as this can only be; you had to be there! Spirit and Creator relates to each of us at our own level and only when we are open in heart to hear. Living in Spirit is living in truth and recognizing that all is only relative to the Creator and the creation.

Thank you Creator and creation for letting me visit this place in my travels through time.

ADDENDUM

Full Circle
What Goes Around – Comes Around!

Some things happen to complete a circle in order that other things can continue to go on. This book was supposed to be complete and yet the circle was not completed so I must share this with you.

An email came in and it said:

> Boozhoo Noodin - Thank you so much for forwarding the ceremonies information. It is, of course, helpful. My passport card arrived this afternoon also.

> I need to tell you now that I am wanting female company for this journey and so if Liz is not coming - and I doubt she is - I'm not sure I'll be going. I have contacted a few women to try and connect with about carpooling and camp sharing for the ceremonies, but I've no news yet. My heart is in these teachings as you well know and it is my desire to shift the way in which I approach these ceremonies; time that I find my way on this path as a woman, without the male energy. I trust Spirit would want it no other way.

> I am telling you now because if we cannot find another woman to travel with us in your vehicle then I won't be going and you may wish to change your plans since I know you were originally trying to accommodate my work schedule (for which I'm very grateful). I'll either have to travel alone or find another ride with mixed or female company.

This choice is for many reasons, all guided by my heart and my prayers are out. It is for the highest.

I trust this day was beautiful for you. I worked in the yard all afternoon while Dee Dee chased the chickens. It was quite funny.

Walking in Beauty.,

Wabishka Maiingun

Considering that this was my best friend and we had recently parted ways due to a new boyfriend in her life, I was deeply saddened by this email. The influence of this new man in her life was obviously ending our ability to even maintain any closeness in our friendship.

The promise to take her to ceremonies did have some restrictions in that I would have to leave late to attend and depart from ceremonies early to get her back home. Now that was washed away with this new development. The ceremony was due to start in three weeks and I would now be able to go on in time to help with the work.

Just at the moment that I read this email the phone rang. It was Nish Nung calling from Lake Lena Rez in Minnesota. When I answered he said: "my Dad has gone over". I was silent for a moment, letting this news soak in. "I know!" I answered. "I will be on the road in the morning and should be there in two days." "Good", he answered and then hung up.

Many things went through my mind after that phone call. An email comes in to tell me I am released from an obligation that would control when I could leave for the west and then I get a call that requires my immediate attention to travel. The separation that was needed between Wabishka Maiingun and me was being enforced even though I had tried hard to keep the connection.

Misho had visited New England just a week or so before. He called me then and was seemingly angry with me when we talked. I did not know why.

He wanted to use the covers from my sweat lodge and wanted me to bring them to him. I went to Wabishka Maiingun's home and picked up the covers and took them to Misho. While visiting with him he would hardly speak to me. He seemed bitterly angry with me but would say nothing and I did not ask. Oshki was there and after awhile I told them I would have to leave and wished them all well..

As Oshki and I walked out of the house where Misho was visiting I told him that something was wrong with Misho. Oshki told me that he had gone to emergency the night before with chest pains but that he was all right and would be fine. I told Oshki that I could see that Misho was leaving us and that I felt I had just said goodbye to my teacher of so many years.

It was the last time that I would see my teacher and I would be contacted by his son Nish Nung the following week.

The night before Nish Nung called I had a dream. In the dream I saw Misho standing in my camp looking at me. He had a smile on his face as if to say everything was good. He was peaceful and was not angry with me anymore.

It was no surprise to me that Misho was gone.

While driving out to Lake Lena my travels were not without incident. It takes twenty two hours to make the drive and I was driving straight through to get there as soon as I could. At about two in the morning I was traveling through Illinois listening to beautiful music on the satellite radio I had just purchased the week before. It was a peaceful ride to that point. All at once my engine suddenly made a bang and then started to rumble and shake the car. I knew the engine had just blown! My thoughts first went to what to do now and then to the question of how to get to Lake Lena.

As I waited for a tow truck I thought about getting to Lake Lena and remembered that Oshki would be coming through about six hours later. I called him and he was on the road about an hour out of New Hampshire. I gave him information on where I would be and he agreed to pick me up.

My native brothers often refer to my Jeep as a wandering wigwam since I travel all over by car and have enough gear to camp anywhere in any season. It was no surprise that the engine blew since the car had two hundred forty thousand miles on it.

The garage wanted to know what to do and I told them to replace the engine. In my financial condition there were not a whole lot of choices. A new car was out of the question.

Oshki would pick me up to go to Lake Lena and then drop me off to pick up the car on his way home. I could continue my trip from there after the ceremony for Misho.

Why now, should the engine go? It had been running well and I always have it checked before I go on the road to make sure everything is right in the vehicle. It is likely that it just wore out and went but what other forces might be at work?

Native teachings often refer to things that happen when someone close passes over. Like there is a series of events that often occur. The breakdown of a vehicle, hitting a deer on the road, a horse dying on the ride and things being lost just when they are needed. Almost as if there has to be an effort made to be where you are called to be. It is as if something is saying slow down, be focused, be determined and finish what you start.

I thought of what Misho would have said; "Just do it!"

Oshki finally showed up about ten hours later.

There were no motels available in the town I was in because of an antique auto show going on so I slept in a park across the street from the garage. Something tapped me and when I opened my eyes there was a local police officer looking down at me. It didn't take much explanation as to why he was there.

"Who are you and why are you sleeping here", the officer asked.

I explained to him that there were no rooms in the town and that my vehicle had broken down during the night. That I was waiting for the garage to open so that I could have mechanics look at my vehicle.

He checked my I.D. and then instructed me to gather my gear and leave the park because people might see me camping and call the police. I agreed and did as I was told.

It was good to travel with Oshki because we had not had a lot of time to visit over the past few years. Oshki, being Misho's adopted son, had a lot of information to share about what might be expected of us when we arrived at Misho's home at Lake Lena. The drive was uneventful but long. Oshki's car was a small Chevy Nova and not nearly as comfortable to ride in as a Jeep Cherokee.

We arrived at Misho's home around three in the morning and a few people were up to greet us as we came in. We went behind the house to the fire and offered our asema. Nish Nung was asleep in one of the bedrooms and we did not want to wake him so we put up our tents in the yard and bedded down for the rest of the night.

In the morning I went with Nish Nung to the place down by the St. Croix River where Misho was born. It was the place that Misho's band of Indians, the Azhimook Band, had lived for many decades in the past. It was quiet now and grown over with bush and forest. The river of water gently flowed by honoring the whole area with a silence and peacefulness.

Nish Nung brought me to a place just a few feet from the pine trees where Misho's parents Wigwam had once been and pointed to the ground. "This is where I want my father buried" he said.

"OK. It will be done." I answered.

We went back to the house and I stayed by the ceremony fire behind the house for a time visiting with all of the family that had come. Nish Nung came by and asked if I would watch the fire at the community house for awhile to give the fire keeper a break. I nodded agreement and drove over to the community center to release the fire keeper.

Around three in the afternoon Oshki came by and picked me up. "We have to go to town to the funeral home." He explained. It was time to prepare Misho. About twenty people were there. Misho's children, cousins, nephews and grand children were gathered.

Nish Nung sat in the room near his father. The room had been smudged with sage and sweet grass. Misho was covered with a sheet to be prepared and dressed for his traveling on into the next realm.

Nish Nung told the women to wait in another room. He instructed Oshki and me to take the sheet off of Misho and some of the men brought in copper bowls containing Cedar Water. Nish Nung instructed each of the men in the room to take a cloth and wet it in the Cedar Water to wash Misho before dressing him. "There are to be no tears" he emphasized. We all did as we were instructed and Misho was cleansed for his journey.

Everyone stood back after the cleansing except Oshki and me. As veterans we were the ones that would stand by Misho.

The women were then invited in to dress Misho. His best clothing was brought in and the women dressed him. He looked so good in his native clothing prepared to travel.

Nish Nung then brought in Misho's pipe and feathers. A ceremony that is ancient and powerful was done to complete the preparation.

We left and Misho was taken to the tribal community center for the ceremony.

That evening Nish Nung and I were in the kitchen at Misho's home alone. Nish Nung told me his dad came back from the east very angry with me. I told Nish Nung that I could feel the anger but did not know what it was about and Misho would not say anything.

Nish Nung explained that Misho's woman friend had told Misho that I was taking advantage of him and exploiting him. "She had poisoned him against you." He said.

When Misho got back to Lake Lena, Nish Nung explained, "I set him straight on what you are doing and how you are helping the people. When he left he was not mad with you anymore."

I answered, "I know! He has told me everything is good between us."

Two of the four days of ceremony were left and Nish Nung asked if I would take the night fire at the community center. I was honored to do this and be close to my teacher.

The first night on the fire many Elders came by and it was good to meet some of them. As the night passed I was able to put down my sleeping bag and rest, waking periodically to check the fire.

At one time that I slept, I dreamt that Misho was talking to me. He told me that when I returned home I was to have a sweat lodge. His instruction was specific. "Do everything yourself from building the lodge, the fire, gathering the grandfathers, pouring the sweat and closing and cleaning after the lodge. Do this within four weeks from now." He concluded.

A grandmother of the Ojibwe from Red Lake Reservation had been asked to oversee the ceremonies for Misho. Her name was Anna and she was a very short woman and needed a walker to move about together with a nurse for assistance. She would drag her feet as she moved around. Anna came to the fire just after sunrise and offered her prayers. She sat down and looked at me for a long time.

"You are the one they call Noodin," Anna said. "You and others in the East have been given many teachings by Nagan We Widung. It is now up to you and those that have been taught to carry those teachings to others. These things were not given to you to keep to yourself. Do you understand?"

I answered her that I do understand.

In the morning twelve of us went to the place by the river where Misho would be buried. We took turns digging and made a hole six feet deep, four feet wide and eight feet long for the casket. The burying place had been made ready.

Each afternoon and evening ceremony was continued at the community center for Misho. On the fourth day a skabewis for Anna came to the fire and asked me if I would let Anna use my drum to sing a personal song for Misho. I took my drum from Oshki's car and gave it to the skabewis.

I could hear Anna singing her song to Misho inside the center. It was almost like listening to a lullaby and lasted for about a half hour.

All other singing used the water drum of the Midewiwin Society for ceremony so the use of a personal song was very special. I was honored that she used my drum.

Toward the evening many of the young ones came out by the fire. They danced and played and sang and told stories way into the night. As it grew late I became very tired and put out my sleeping bag to rest by the fire. Soon I was asleep despite the commotion going on around me. Later, around midnight, I awoke to check the fire. I could see that Oshki had come in to the fire and put down his sleeping bag. He was sleeping to the south of the fire and I to the west.

Someone had brought the feast meal left over's out and put them into the fire. There was so much that it was out and around the edge of the fire. I built the fire and put as much of it as I could into the fire to burn. In the dark it was hard to see if I had cleaned it up properly. Later that night I awoke enough to notice someone was near the fire but fell back to sleep.

Near morning I heard something. It was an Owl giving its call but it was different and woke me completely. The Barred Owl gave its call almost in a whisper rather than a strong call as one might hear in the night. It is unusual to me to hear a barred so late or close to dawn.

I started to close my eyes and go back to sleep when something seemed to touch my head. It was moist as if I had been licked by something. I looked up and could see three dogs standing a few feet away between the fire and the community center. As I looked I could see that they looked more like wolves than dogs. Their tails were down and loose rather than curled and their legs were long. The one closest to me was white and the other two were dark colored. They stood there just looking at me. I could not believe what I was seeing.

I sat up a little to get a better look and the three of them immediately turned and trotted around the side of the community center building. They were gone. It was no use to get up and try to follow. I knew they would be long gone before I could get out of my sleeping bag.

I did get up though and built up the fire, straightening out the food mess as best I could. It looked better than the night before as if someone had cleaned it more during the night. After building the fire I went into the community center and over to where Misho was. An elder woman sat next to Misho doing some craft work. Her name was Paula and she was Misho's cousin. I went and sat by her.

"You live in this community don't you, Paula?" I asked. She indicated that she did. "Are there any large dogs running at night here that you know of?"

She replied, "No large ones. There are some small dogs that run wild here but no large ones."

I asked, "Have any wolves been seen around here?"

Answer, "Not on the rez but up on highway 41 they have been spotted. They say there are three that are up there. Why do you ask?"

I was hesitant to answer. I did not want to sound silly and doubted that anyone would believe me. I slowly began to tell her what had happened; "I was sleeping and was awakened by an owl calling out softly. It woke me from a dead sleep. A close friend has Owl as her helper and so it alerted me because I thought of her when I heard it. As I went back to sleep something licked me on the top of my head. When I looked around I saw three wolves. Two dark and the one closest was white. When I pushed myself up from the ground they left."

Paula made no visible response. Looking at her work she only told me that it could have been.

I got up and went back out to the fire. I wished I had not told her and decided I would not mention it again. One of Misho's helpers was white wolf. My friend that I sorely missed is called Maiingun Wabishka, white wolf. Nish Nung also has the helper of white wolf. It was a lot to think about.

I continued to take care of the fire and Oshki got up. I said nothing of the incident and he was unaware of anything strange. At that time an uncle of Nish Nung's came to the fire. He is a very experienced traditional Indian and dedicated as a fire keeper. He asked if I had heard him come to the fire during the night. I told him I knew someone had come by. "I cleaned the fire and picked up some of the food that had not burned." He said. "I don't know who taught you fire keeping but it is your responsibility to see that the fire is cared for properly."

I thanked him for his criticism and assured him that I would do better. He was courteous and went on with his business.

Paula came out from the lodge shortly after that and sat by the fire. She asked, "Noodin, did you see some Elders leave the center last night as you came in to talk to me?"

I told her that I saw no one.

She went on; "They just came by again and told me that as they were driving away from the center they saw three wolves run across the road. Those must be the wolves that visited you."

Wow! Validated! I felt better and yet still could not believe what had happened. So much to ponder.

Nish Nung came by a few minutes later. "You saw a white wolf last night while at the fire." He said.

I told him I had and he asked; "Did you see me?"

I told him I did not.

He answered, "I was standing on the other side and saw him too."

Nish Nung and I are like brothers and I was grateful for his confirmation as well.

The day went on and Misho was put onto his journey to the next place. A circle completed and another begins. There is no end to the cycles of life and the teachings that are passed on. My guide moved to another realm but he has not left. He visits me often and sometimes daily as he does with many and is as close now as he was in a physical way during his life cycle here. He shared with me the medicine teachings of the shield and those teachings have become my teacher.

Miigwich Nagan We Widung!

GLOSSARY

Ojibway Words

Aanii ezha a ya yaan	How are you?
Amik	beaver
ahow, aho, howaa	form of acknowledgement
Anishinabe	Indian
Asema	ah-say-maa / tobacco
at'i zookan	stories of the people
azhaamook	Cross Roads
bamaagaana	by adoption
bimadiziwin	life
booshoo	greetings
bungii et'igo	just a little bit
chimookamon	chi-moo-ka-mon / long knife
d'baad end'zin	humility
de we igon	drum
debwe win	*Truth*
dibit	Night
dibwewin	di bway win, truth

gana wa ba ne	we see you
giindash	and you
giizhikandug	gee zhi ka dug – white cedar
Gi zhi Manidoo	Great Spirit
gowiin	gow ween, no
gwe kwaad ziwin	honesty
indizhinikaz	what I am called
indodiem	my clan
indo	I can
indow	I am
ishkode inninee	ish-ko-day i-ni-nee / fire keeper
Ishkwan diem	ish-kwan-dame / door
Maang	Loon
Maiingun	*wolf*
mashkode bizhiki	buffalo
m'naa den d'mowin	respect
Medewiwin	Medicine Society
mino giizhigut	it is a good day
mi gi zee	bald eagle
miigas	me-gaas / Conch shell
miigwich	Thank you
miishiikenh	turtle
mi-no-gee-zhi-gut	it is a good day

miximong	Divers
mukwaa	bear
mushkadebug	moosh ka day bug – sage
nagaan-way-widong	First to Speak, First Thunder
nbaa kaa win	wisdom
nichomis	Grandmother
nikaang	my brother
nimii nu ayaa	I am fine
nish nung	two stars
niswii miikanung	three paths
Noodin	Wind/air
Ogichidaa	veteran
Ojibwemowin	Ojibway language
Oshki	new
ozhibige Inini	writing man
Potowatomy	Tribe in the Ojibwe Nation
sabe	wild man
shkitaagan	birch fungas
skabewis	helper
umbe	Go
wabiigwan	flower
wawa kay shee	deer
wabishka	*white*

weno booshoo	name of first man
wiinagush	wee na goosh – sweet grass
zaa gidwin	love
zhaganaashi	English
zhinqwak	White Pine
zoon gide'iwin	bravery

REVIEWS

"Something a little different and refreshing in its honesty, this journey with Noodin in finding and traveling the Red Road is an enlightening experience. By sharing his love and energy while seeking his Spiritual connection, we each have the opportunity to learn a bit more about our own journey through this existence, here and now. I have been privileged to personally hear my good friend share some of the teachings through his telling of the legends, and can relate them to many of the lessons I have been given while on my own Sacred Path. You are welcomed to these wonderful experiences, page by page, and blessed by the story Noodin brings to help you discover your own. I found this an inspiring read, and one destined to bring understanding to many who are seeking the truth in their lives."

- Noreen Powers - Medicine Crow Woman,
Northern Cheyanne

"It is powerful! It is heartfelt and it is genuine. I sit here with huge tears running down my cheeks. I cannot believe the pages you wrote when I knew you so long ago have become a manifestation of the dream you used to talk about."

- Kathe, Kathleen Dumont, LADC, LCPC, CCS -

"I love how in your story, of many stories, so many teachings are interwoven and how, on many levels, the teachings are on many levels, going so much deeper than meets the eye:"

-Blessings to you, Donna Packard, M. Ed.

"Miigwech brother for being who you are. Your strength is admirable. I enjoyed reading your manuscript."

-Josephine Mandamin, National Grandmother
Ojibwe First Nation, Canada

"I think it will build a much needed bridge between our cultures."

- Peter Schuler, Ojibwe First Nation, Canada

Made in the USA
San Bernardino, CA
06 November 2014